一个意大利记者眼中的

北京

(1976—2008)

AN EYE-WITNESS OF AN ITALIAN JOURNALIST IN
BEIJING

[意]阿德里亚诺·马达罗 著/摄 陆辛 译

人民出版社

我眼中的马达罗（代序）

1986 年初我在北京国际饭店工作，任餐饮部副经理，主管西餐和酒吧业务。一天总经理把我找去，说意大利著名的"图拉"餐馆集团通过一位热心的意大利朋友找到中国驻米兰领馆，愿意和北京国际饭店合资经营意大利餐厅，定于一个月后来华洽谈此事，特别提到这位意大利朋友，叫Màdaro，是一位意大利记者，也是中国驻意大利使领馆的老朋友，曾多次来华，写了不少正面宣传中国的书籍。一个月后，在北京饭店我见到了这位意大利朋友。他的个头不是很高，但是他那风度翩翩的举止和那双炯炯有神的眼睛，给我留下深刻的印象。我们最早的接触是从起名字开始的，他让我给他起个贴切的中国名字，这对我这个学拉丁语言的人来说不难，稍加思考，一个和意大利语发音接近又很上口的中国名字出现了，马达罗，他非常满意这个名字，因为按照中国属性，他是属马的，后来我就干脆叫他老马了。没想到这个老马，竟成了我的好朋友，国内国外，风风雨雨，一下子20多年过去了，从1976年老马第一次来中国到2008年的32年里，老马前后来中国155次，竟有140次是由我陪伴他的，平均每隔两个月就能见面。如果我忙或者在国外，他是不来中国的。

老马是个记者，他非常热爱中国的历史文化，他可以准确地说出中国各个朝代的起始时间和发生的重大事件，甚至皇帝的名字、年号、庙号，以及生卒年月都记得清清楚楚。而让我最为感动的是他对老北京历史文化的喜爱和崇拜，达到了如痴如醉、登峰造极的程度，也许就是这个原因把我们捆绑在了一起。开始，我并不是个老北京迷，在中学和大学，我的历史成绩是最差的，特别是经过"文化大革命"，脑子里对过去是一片空白，而真正改变我，把我"拖下水"的是老马。理由很简单，面对着一位来自数千公里以外的意大利人，向你如数家珍地讲述着辉煌悠久的中华文明史，而你作为一个中国人却显得如此的无知和渺小，自然很惭愧啊！后来我们就有了本书老马文字中提到的情节。那时，我们的交通工具主要是骑自行车，乘公共汽车和火车。无论刮风下雨，无论严寒酷暑，我们走遍了北京，走遍了全国，拍摄了数万张照片，收集了数千册有关风景、古建筑以及文物的书籍和画册。

那时的中国还没有完全开放，一个中国人带一个欧洲老外，背个相机、摄像机大街小巷地转悠和拍摄，可想而知有多困难。友善，好奇，拒绝，回避，警惕，监视，我们在这些表情和目光注视下，记录了当时最真实的镜头。一次在外地拍摄录像，我和老马被请进当地派出所，被警察询问了4个多钟头才放出来，原因是当地群众举报老马拍摄了一个小孩向他要钱的镜头，而老马又是意大利人，他们把他当作安东尼奥尼了*。这个真实的故事，今天听起来很可笑，可是20年前、30年前在中国是经常发生的。

---

* 米开朗基罗·安东尼奥尼（1912—2007），意大利电影大师，一生创作了25部电影和众多剧本。1972年他来到中国，拍摄了纪录片《中国》，记录了1972年中国的城市和乡村。

老马不是专业摄影师，他的作品谈不上有多高的艺术水平。他是个记者，作家，也是一个非常热爱中国，特别是北京的外国人。他的镜头始终对准普普通通的百姓，作品反映的是真实的百姓生活。1990年后，老马拍的作品明显减少，用他的话讲，找不到他所喜欢的感觉了，到处是高楼大厦，现代化了。

不知为什么，老马对北京有如此深厚的感情：老北京的消失，他痛心；新北京的建立，他为之骄傲。"非典"来了，他难过，特地从意大利赶到中国参加抗击"非典"的斗争。真如他所说，北京是他的第二故乡。每次乘飞机从国外或者外地回到北京，当他看到机场高速收费口的古牌楼建筑时，就激动不已，我坐在他旁边，足能体会他的那种感受。

以前，老马的作品多是在意大利出版。2003年起，经已故的国内著名的意大利文学翻译家吕同六先生的介绍，老马结识了人民出版社的编辑林敏，出版了他的第一本关于北京的中文译本：《1900年的北京》。这本书是老马根据当年意大利驻华公使朱塞佩·萨尔瓦戈·拉吉侯爵留下的外交皮箱中的珍贵资料而编写的，书中采用大量的历史照片形象、真实地介绍了100多年前北京发生的这场历史事件，许多资料是从未发表过的。正因为如此，2008年国家大剧院上演话剧《天朝1900》时，经老马授权，从该书珍贵的历史照片中选取了百幅珍品举办了"1900的北京"图片展，受到了观众的热烈欢迎。本书是出版计划的第二本书，根据林敏编辑的策划创意而编排，入选了新闻出版署"纪念改革开放30周年百种图书"。本书在中国的出版采用中英文对照的方式；在意大利的出版，则采用的是意大利文和英文对照的方式。为了充分地表达作者老马的真实思想，我尽可能地根据意大利文原意，参照英文稿的翻译表达方式进行翻译和整理。我们在工作中得到了鲁岚峰、李玉成、陈伯祥等老师们的热心指导。明年计划出的第三本书：《1839年前的北京》（暂定），是根据老马收藏的有关那个时期的西洋版画和西方造访者的文章来描绘一个康乾盛世的北京，一个在西方人眼里神奇的北京，一个未遭受外国蹂躏的北京。

老马的中国之行在继续着，他对中国的热情和关注在继续着，他和人民出版社的合作也在继续着。我们有理由相信中国越来越扎根在他的心灵深处。用他自己的话来说，他的前生是一个中国人。

陆　辛 *

二〇〇八年十月

---

* 陆辛，毕业于北京大学西语系。曾在国旅做过导游，在北京国际饭店餐饮部当过经理。后在意大利留学。回国后，在意大利某服装集团任驻华首席代表。现在自己开设一家公司，专门从事有关中国和意大利两国文化交流和贸易的工作。

目　录

见证北京

32 年前，从意大利来北京是很困难的。我乘坐每周只有一班的班机从巴黎起飞，飞越了意大利、阿尔巴尼亚、伊朗、巴基斯坦和喜马拉雅山脉，最终从新疆进入中国境内。飞机抵达北京的时间比原计划晚了近一个小时。当时已经是晚上 8 点，天很黑了。在北京上空飞行和降落的过程中，窗外看不到任何灯光，我感觉自己来到了地球上一个很遥远的角落。当我走下舷梯步行穿过停机坪时，闻到的是机场上散发的航空汽油味，然而给我印象最深的是候机楼里悬挂的一幅映照在昏暗灯光下的巨幅毛泽东画像。一片黑暗中，头顶上的星星显得格外明亮。如此美丽的星空，在以后我再来北京时是不多见的。

我乘坐的飞机是中国航空公司波音 707 型客机，飞行了近 20 个小时，只在卡拉奇做了短暂的停留。机舱里乘客秩序井然，他们个子都比较矮，身着蓝色或黑色制服，头戴同样颜色的帽子，女士们也穿着同样颜色的衣服，让我很难区分乘客的性别。

在北京机场的通道口，有两位年轻的机场服务小姐示意我到机场休息室休息，她们都身穿淡蓝色套装，脚上是黑色搭襻儿白塑料底的布鞋。休息室里散发着浓郁的茉莉花香水味，摆着几张考究的皮质大沙发，略显陈旧，但每个沙发背上都铺着白色棉钩织品，更显示出它的尊贵。这是间贵宾室，墙上挂着两幅巨大的装裱精致的中国书法作品。低矮的茶几上整齐地码放着一排带盖的茶杯，茶杯的中间有一只红色烤漆大暖水瓶和一只插着紫玫瑰的玻璃花瓶。这种细微的温馨，

— • 1 • —

不仅使人感觉不到革命年代的火药味，反而形象地预示我的此行会有好运气。两位小姐带着焦虑的神情回来，用蹩脚的英语向我解释说，因为时间太晚，今晚我不能进城了，没有出租车，也找不到任何可以送我进城的汽车，现在她们唯一可以做的，就是安排我到餐厅用晚餐。我们没有经过行李厅，直接到了贵宾室，所以我不知道我的行李在哪儿，也许压根儿就没有行李提取处。不过，此时我更关心的问题是我今晚要在哪儿过夜。

这就是1976年4月29日的夜晚，在等待了多年并经过这漫长的飞行之后，我到达了一个既神秘又"封闭的"还笼罩着毛泽东革命神话的中国的心脏。气味，空气中散发出的文化大革命的硝烟气味，很像煤油和茉莉花的味道。说老实话，我还闻到一股大蒜味。这是从两位年轻小姐口中呼出的，因我盯着她们脖子后那两根摆来摆去的又黑又粗的辫子，一直跟在她们后面走。我终于成功地来到了这个闭关自守的国度，激动和喜悦之情溢于言表，顺其自然地接受了这几个小时在我身边发生的一切。

机场餐厅里有几张大圆桌，靠墙站着近10位女服务员。她们身穿白色工作服，站成一排，看见我进来，赶忙招呼我在一个大桌子旁坐下。桌上摆放着10套餐具。我好奇地环顾四周，没有见到别的什么人，只有我一人。我确实感到意外，这可是在大革命的年代里，却能有这么多的年轻姑娘为一个人服务，真不可想象，也许因为我是远道而来的客人？我一点儿不懂中文，那两位年轻小姐也没有帮我翻译。后来，服务员从厨房端来了数量多得吓人的饭菜，我想她们以为会有10人用餐。这么丰盛的菜肴，我一个人怎能吃下？10个煎蛋，3盘肉菜，3盘海鲜，还有3盘蔬菜，另加一盆米饭，一堆像小山似的馒头外加10瓶啤酒。守候在我周围的10位天使般的服务员对我的胃口大失所望。我情不自禁地笑了，我应该把这些像宴会上的佳肴打包带走。

吃完晚饭，两位年轻小姐返回来带我去休息，我说时候尚早，是否可以去机场看看。看得出来，她们对于我这么晚不睡觉的要求感到吃惊（已是晚9点），示意我跟她们走。在机场大厅，我看到许多上夜班的工人，看上去他们都是一些十几岁的年轻人，正在召开革命会议。大家盘腿坐在地上，手持著名的小红宝书，在激烈地讨论着什么。一座巨大的毛主席塑像在注视着整个大厅，塑像周围摆满了鲜花。我问这群年轻人为什么如此激动，在讨论着什么？他们中有一个人会讲英语，对我说，他们在讨论明天由谁去担任机场管理的负责人。那么，我是不是可以问问他们我的行李在哪儿？可转念一想，在中国首都机场，在他们召开无产阶级革命会议的时候，我提如此无足轻重的问题是否体现了我的资产阶级利己主义思想？

候机楼通往市中心的林荫大道两旁种满了杨树。我来到马路右边一个兵营，一名站岗的士兵在照看我的行李。看来这里就是今晚我入住的酒店，在营房的门口，那两位年轻小姐向我鞠躬告别，在东方国家，鞠躬是一种礼节，不是卑屈。她们还说明天早上7点钟会有人叫早，并且陪我到刚才吃晚饭的地方用早餐。什么时候进北京？答曰早饭之后会有人来带我进城。我提着行李刚刚走进一间不大的房间，身后房门立即被反锁上。房间里的两张铁床让我想起了老式医院，铁床上分别铺着粉色和蓝色的绣花被，在一张小木桌子上，摆着几只带盖的茶杯和一个装满开水的暖瓶。有两把扶手椅，扶手椅背上也铺着白色棉编织品，一个三条腿的木制挂衣架，这些就是这房间所有的家具。一扇小铁门的后面是间不大的厕所，有一个挂了黄色水锈的马桶。窗户上像牢房一样装着铁条，只挂了一对绣着牡丹花的浅色窗帘。我马上意识到，明晨5点，阳光就会照到窗帘上，光线会刺醒我。现在是晚上10点，夜深人静，我得赶紧上床，很快便进入了梦乡。在中国度过的第一个晚上，我睡得很香，很多年来我都没有睡过这么好。如果不是第二天早上被窗外的广播喇叭播放的音乐吵醒，我还不知要睡到几点呢！我从床上爬起来，拉开洒满阳光的窗帘，看到了窗外穿着短裤和背心的军人，他们在整齐地出操，有节奏地高喊"一、二、三、一、二、三"，同时还不时地高呼"毛主席万岁！"这句在当时家喻户晓的口号。

一个个头比较矮的男子向我走来。他身穿蓝色制服，扣子一直扣到脖子下面，上衣的口袋里插着一只钢笔，轻声地对我说："先生，您好！"他微笑着，露出一口不整齐的牙齿，头发精心修剪过，一双惺忪的睡眼有点儿肿。我忽然意识到，这就是国际旅行社委派给我的翻译。他直截了当地自我介绍。他说他是范同志，称呼他范就行了，

他的任务是尽责尽心地让我在北京的日子过得愉快；接着他又以严肃而和蔼的口吻告诉我，根据中华人民共和国法律，在中国哪些事可以做，哪些事不可以做。我知道这是他的工作，不过我很

马达罗与范翻译的合影

喜欢他流露出的那种无奈的表情。如何让他和我一起，协助我深入地去探索这个国家呢？范接着告诉我要住的酒店叫新侨饭店，位于市中心，是苏联帮助建造的，酒店的条件非常舒适。后来我才知道，新侨饭店所在的这条街当年在义和团运动时期，曾经是外国使馆区，但范小心翼翼地避开了这个话题。他只是告诉我，新侨饭店三楼有家北京独一无二的西餐厅，但只供应早餐。他表示，他会陆续解答我感兴趣的问题，并向我保证，他会陪着我，形影不离。接着他把我介绍给我们的司机，司机见到我就像见到老朋友一样，客气地问候我"你好"。"你好"这句话很快就进入到我的口语中。

从机场通往北京市区的马路比乡间的沥青路宽不了多少，路边种了两排白杨树，形成一条绿

色长廊，道路中间缓慢地行驶着马车、手推车和卡车，偶尔能见到几辆小轿车。每当通过喧闹的十字路口，四方抢行的车辆总让人感到似乎要发生交通事故，然而让人庆幸的是有惊无险，接着他们又在漫天飞舞的杨絮中继续缓慢地前行。路的两边是精心耕种的农田，远远望去，很像一个巨大的家庭菜园子，但是我见不到任何房屋和村庄，只看到一群群在黄土地上辛勤耕作的农民，微风掀起阵阵尘土，一面面红旗随风飘扬。到北京郊区时，路边出现了一些低矮的土坯房，房顶上覆盖着破旧的灰瓦，还可以看到一些墙面剥落的简易楼房，看得出是出自于非专业的泥瓦工之手。幸好四周绿色的大自然春意盎然，给我平添了几分好感，舒缓了远处大槐树树荫下的那些灰色矮平房带给我的压抑不安的心情。我不知不觉地置身于神秘的北京之中。我感觉到这里充满绿色，它压倒了其他景色。我们越往城里走，树木就越多地覆盖着房子，只能隐约看见灰色的围墙和带翘角小屋顶的油漆门。到处是人群，街上充满了熙熙攘攘的市民，所有的业务和活动都在街上进行，仿佛大街是他们的生活舞台，而那些低矮的房子只不过是日常生活演出中的幕布而已。绵延不断的自行车、手推车、马车、按喇叭的卡车、拥挤的公交车、背包的步行者，站在家门口等人或好奇消遣的平民百姓，我真难以想象这就是北京。我感到我是在穿过一座既熟悉又陌生的城市；它的农村面貌，布满灰尘的街道，简陋的建筑，身穿蓝色棉服的乱哄哄的人群，稀少的有特色或有纪念性的建筑，在安静连绵的槐树的轻盈树冠覆盖下，景物时隐时现，这一切都使人感到这只不过是农村郊区，而并非一个首都，触摸不到中国首都跳动的心脏。在人口众多的辽阔郊区，感觉不到制度管理上的威严和军队方面的傲慢。红色中国首都以没有武装、人性化和友善的方式向我问候，它那松懈平和的常态使我感到惊奇。我们驶进一条宽阔的林荫道后，我的朋友范马上告诉我，它便是通向天安门广场的神话般的、意为永久和平的长安街。长安街两旁依然是被槐树簇拥着的灰色低矮的房子，只是马路上车辆多了些。随后，我们拐入王府井大街。王府井大街是这座城市最重要的商业街，街头耸立着高大的北京饭店。在这条街上，我终于看到了一些有特色的建筑。这里，人群聚集在沿着两旁种了树的人行道上，商店里顾客盈门。我们经过一座天主教堂，这就是赫赫有名的东堂，高大坚固的围墙紧紧包围着它。再往前走，可以见到美术馆顶上的黄色琉璃瓦。最后我们停在了一座只有三个侧面的俄式建筑前。这种难看的建筑外形，在20世纪50年代的东欧国家很流行。

这是一座接待海外华人的酒店，名叫"华侨大厦"。我之所以要在这里下车，为的是去签证办公室接受护照检查。怪哉！没有人问我昨天晚上住在哪儿。下车伊始，先闻到了一股炒米饭的味道。穿过大堂，范带我到了签证处，那里的人用茶招待我们。手续办得很快，范也不知和里面的官员说了些什么，惹得那官员哈哈大笑，最后官员用双手把护照递还给我。这种递名片的姿势，中国人依然保留到今天。一切都很顺利，现在我已经取得了合法居留权，我要回我的酒店了。32年弹指一挥间，我一直想重新踏上当年我进入北京走过的第一个台阶，但是到了20世纪90年代，这家饭店已经修缮一新，变成了一个现代五星级的豪华酒店，也成了我在北京的常驻寓所。

新侨饭店*在崇文门旁边，离北京火车站不远，崇文门可惜在1969年被拆除了。我的房间朝南，正对着北京的外城。这家酒店之所以出名，是因为爱德华·斯诺曾在这里住过。斯诺是一位著名的美国记者，也是《红星照耀中国》一书的作者。在20世纪30年代，他冲破蒋介石国民党的层层封锁，到了延安，谒见毛泽东主席和革命红军。60年代和70年代，他又受到毛泽东的邀请，重返中国，一直住在这里。在整个文化大革命期间，新侨饭店居住的都是对中国革命持友好态度国家的代表团。这里的服务员都接受过西方礼仪训练，知道"野蛮"的外国客人的古怪习惯，比如说外国人吃饭要用刀叉，衬衫和长裤要熨平，在电话挂不通时使用电报等等。一眨眼的工夫，我就到了房间。房间的钥匙是铜的，沉甸甸的，还挂了个很大的铝合金牌，上面有"新侨饭店"四个红色大字。热情的范带我到了位于大堂角落的邮局，在那里我发了电报，电报内容是：我已到北京，ok，天气很好。到了晚上，我想给家人打个电话，却发现房间里没有电话机。后来才知道我必须到我的楼层服务台登记，由服务员与电话员

预约。楼层服务台在走廊尽头，那里有烧开水的锅炉和电话。我拿着护照，填了一张表，然后就回房间几乎等了一整夜，盼望着服务员跑来敲我的门。终于等来了服务员。他告诉我不知摇了多少次铃，总算拨通了经西伯利亚到意大利的电话。在那个年代，用手机打长途，简直是匪夷所思，甚至你想躺在舒适的软床上用房间的座机电话打长途，都十分困难。现在，我考虑的问题是，如何尽快地深入到北京老百姓日常生活中去呢？看来一切都要指望单纯可爱的范了。后来，有一次他去意大利出差，受到我全家的热情款待。

我同意范的常规日程的安排，每天上午8点，当司机来时，我已经准备好出发。此外，我还想自己出去了解一些与众不同的，或者非官方开放的地方。当时的北京，吃过晚饭7点半后，街上几乎看不到行人，餐厅、电影院和剧场都基本上在晚8点关门，没有出租车，饭店房间里没有电视机。一人独自漫步在街头会有些凄凉，偶尔会见到几辆从农村来的马车，停在菜市场前卸菜。因此我常常晚上9点前睡觉，第二天拂晓就起床，有时5点都不到。起来后匆匆用冷水（这个时段不供应热水）洗个澡，用暖壶里的热水刮刮胡子，然后穿上衣服，挎上和我形影不离的莱卡相机出门。因为天刚蒙蒙亮，饭店的夜间值班员奇怪地瞧着我，然后很有礼貌地打招呼："你好！"

北京帝王时期的老地图深深地印在我脑海里。现在的北京地理布局和那时比变化不大。除

---

* 马达罗首次来京（1976年）下榻新侨饭店，但必须先到华侨大厦一层的签证办公室接受护照检查。

了鞑靼城墙＊和大多数城门被拆掉外，北京城基本没有什么变化，多数古建筑保留了下来。虽然很多寺庙变成了学校、工厂和仓库，但它们的地点没有变，依然留在我记忆中的位置上。那数不清的胡同，星罗密布的大街小巷，"鞑靼城"和"汉人城"＊＊之间的网状连接，完美无缺。这就是北京百姓的生活基础。70年代中期我去北京的时候，每天早上，我都习惯独自在北京的心脏地区漫游，原来陌生的城市，如今却如此的亲近，带着毫无戒备的诚意呈现于面前。虽说是一个人独来独往，但并不感觉到孤独，因为处处都有友好的当地居民，他们好奇地看着我拍照摄影，并不认为我这个老外的相机镜头妨碍了他们的生活。我越接近北京人的日常生活，就越喜欢北京人独有的特点，比如北京人即使穷，也总是要显出他们高贵的气质，无论从事什么职业，都喜欢别人称他"爷"。去上学的孩子们带着小马扎，因为当时学校还很穷，没有配备足够的椅子。老人们悠闲地抽着长长的烟袋锅，妇女们忙于干家务活，街上小商贩叫卖着他们的商品，店铺的老板招呼我进他那不太宽敞的铺子逛逛，房子的主人们友好地向我比画着手势，让我跨过门槛，到他们的"四合院"里做客。"四合院"是一种四方形的庭院，是典型的老北京住宅。他们热情地招待我喝茶，嗑葵瓜子。那时的北京不剩别的，就剩胡同，有的是胡同。我也成了"胡同串子"，漫无目标地串。北京人的友好热情，打动了我的心，几乎使我掉下了热泪。他们总是笑嘻嘻的，从不与人作对，就连当时尚存的最后一批红卫兵也不例外。他们自豪地把红袖章戴在胳膊上，虽不能行使任何的权力，但仍是体现着爱国主义的象征，对此我十分容易理解。在这个漫长的春天，毛泽东还健在，人们到处可以感受到他的身影。对他的个人崇拜达到了顶峰，在人们心中他已完全被神化。毛泽东慈祥的面容不仅出现在天安门城楼上，同时也出现在所有的公共建筑物上，他总是注视着他的臣民，让他们既安心又敬畏。

拼音是使用罗马字母和发音拼出汉字的音标，当时汉语拼音已经普及，所以街道和胡同的中文名称上都有相应的拼音，这很便于我学习汉字。首先我从方位词开始学起。在中国，方位词是五个而不是四个，因为除了东、南、西、北外还有中。中，是至关重要的，比如说天安门就是北京的中心。我在北京问路，从来不会问向左或向右，而是问向北或向南，或者问市中心在哪个方向，因为我的宾馆离天安门广场不远。今天依然如此，看着路标，我会准确地告知你所处的位置，是在南、北，还是在东、西。我的方法很简单，比方说我现在在安定门内南大街，如果要返回饭店，只要找到崇文门内北大街就可以了，因为我的酒店位于崇文门内北大街和东便门内西大街的交汇处。我经常做这种辨别方向的练习：观察太阳的位置，从北京平房灰色的屋顶上，辨别

＊指老北京内城，因老北京内城是在元代建的，马可·波罗曾到过这里，在他的"游记"中，他称这座城为"鞑靼城"，明朝在元代城墙的基础上改建成后来的明清两代的北京内城。可西方人还是喜欢称其为"鞑靼城"。

＊＊指北京外城，清代时，汉人必须住在外城，西方人习惯称其为"汉人城"。

出那个最高的金黄色琉璃瓦顶就是故宫，这样很容易找到回宾馆的路。而现在已经不可能了。那个年代的北京，能高过故宫太和殿的建筑寥寥无几，只要角度对，我经常可以透过绿色的树丛，看到故宫金黄色的瓦顶。我的记忆里，永远印着这样一幅壮丽的景观：夕阳西下，绿茵中的宫殿瓦顶闪闪发光，仿佛镀上了一层灿烂的金黄色，宛如一只巨大的盛满菠菜的大碗上面放着一个巨大的煎鸡蛋。

那时北京人的生活，像乡村一样简朴。在早上和下午上下班的高峰期间，大街上可以看到潮水般的自行车洪流，数不清的车铃发出丁零零有节奏的悦耳声。清晨，经常能看见老人们在公园里或在街边练操，打太极拳，另外一些人在舞剑，他们挥舞系着红丝带的木制宝剑；而年轻人则在庄严的进行曲中练功习武，犹如在和一个假想中的敌人搏斗。那时的出租车很少，而且不可以在马路上停车载客。如果要用车的话，只能到北京几家屈指可数的宾馆去办理包车手续，一般是包一整天或数天。在那时，人们一般推荐外国人到宾馆就餐，原因之一是那里的菜肴更"国际化"，而所谓的"国际化菜肴"是指有更多的选择，可选粤菜或川菜，外国人比较喜欢这些口味，因为这些菜与北京的风味菜有很大的不同。在我看来，北京有一家不错的饭店，那是一家位于西单路口的伊斯兰风味餐厅，我常去那里，它离我经常光顾的书店很近。而我每次去，他们都热情相待，招呼我到二楼用餐，那里的餐桌铺着台布，而且可以喝到冰镇啤酒，这是对外国人的一个特例，当时大部分中国人都不爱喝特别凉的饮料，哪怕是在盛夏酷暑，他们爱喝开水，有时还往开水里加些盐。

在故宫空旷的庭院里，游客们带着惊奇的目光注视一切，他们用农民般粗糙的大手摸一摸金漆柱子，敲一敲带有祥云大龙图案的大石雕。游人穿着棉衣，梦幻般地漫游在这块曾被脚穿丝锦鞋的皇帝们踩过的土地，如此的富丽堂皇让他们惊叹不已。也许他们在思考，眼前宫殿中的宝座，就是曾经被他们推翻的旧封建神权的象征，而今却让他们望而生畏，神色迷茫不安。显而易见，他们沐浴在这庄严神圣的气氛中，却听着舒缓悠扬的音乐。音乐声在巨大的天花板和地面之间回荡，并飘荡到宽大庭院的各个角落，最后消失在门外影壁上的那些张牙舞爪的巨龙旁。我注视着这些漫步在金碧辉煌宫殿群中的朴实农民，他们的神色是严肃、崇敬的。宫殿和农民，如此完美的一幕震撼着我，激起我极大的拍摄热情，我的镜头对准了选中的任一目标迅速地进行抓拍。可爱的范望着我，感到莫名其妙：为何故宫遥远的过去让我这样一个外国人如此着迷？我给他解释，古代的工匠们建造了一座完美和谐的建筑群，在我看来，她是古代中华文明的经典杰作。他笑了笑，理解我为什么如此赞美中国的"过去"，而他还得批判"过去"，因为在那时候，消除过去的封建意识的影响是政治需要。随着文化大革命接近尾声，以及毛泽东主席身体的每况愈下，一切都停止了。我预感会发生重大事件，人们在担心会发生什么意外，然而却没发生。1976年春天，在"伟大舵手"去世前的 5 个月里，北京被一种无疼痛感觉的麻木气氛所笼罩。

一次去长城的浏览使我加深了对郊区农村的了解。一条古时留下的老路蜿蜒在春意盎然的山脉中。我们穿过几个像鲁迅笔下描述的村庄。当时八达岭的游客稀少，小商贩更少，眼前一派雄伟而自然的风光。游客多数是来自外地乡下的农民。他们的眼中流露出谨慎和惊奇，注视着我这样一个外国人。他们带着许多干粮，可爱的孩子们穿着花布棉袄，不难看出，这些农民来自这个广袤无际的国家的一些偏远地区。雄伟险峻的长城令人惊叹。我站在那里，在我的脚下、我的眼前，伟大的长城蜿蜒起伏在崇山峻岭中，这是一个坚韧不拔捍卫和平的民族象征。"不到长城非好汉"，毛泽东在长征中写下了这一著名的词句，寓意着一种精神，以长城为象征的一种伟大国家的民族精神。在后来的岁月里，当中国向国际旅游者开放之后，我去长城的次数少了，我对她的神秘感逐渐消失。一批批背包游客的涌入，八达岭变成了一个充满了小商贩的旅游商品市场。当然，这是另一种新的开放形式，但是我还是非常怀念最初到长城的日子，我喜欢那些充满了长征精神奋力攀登长城的农民游客。这是我数年前独自登长城时留下的最深印象，这些印象就如同照片，至今还仍然活生生地印在我心里。这种感觉，就如同我游览过的北京其他地方一样，从天坛到颐和园，我所见到的北京人都极大地影响着我对人生的理解。让我深为感动的是：他们没有任何排外情绪，他们用善良和纯朴，真心欢迎一个来自遥远西方的外来客。

1977 年我第二次去中国的时候，从长城返回北京时才发现，我在长城箭楼上丢失了随身携带的两台照相机中的一台相机。为此，范严肃地责怪我的粗心。翌日下午，当我从香山回来，打开房门时，我吃惊地发现前一天在长城已经"丢失"的那台柯尼卡相机就摆放在桌上。相机旁，有一张英文字条，上面写着："亲爱的朋友，请您保管好自己的财物，万一不慎丢失，请您务必记住丢失在什么地方，这样有人捡到后可以归还给您。您如果不能带着您自己的物品回国，那将多么扫兴呀。"我惊讶得说不出话来，世上有什么地方能发生这种事？中国是一个什么样的国家？中国给我上了一课。后来我向范先生讲述发生的事，顺便问他我的照相机是如何找到的，他们怎么知道是我的相机，如何送还给我的。我的愕然惊奇的表情，使范先生笑得前俯后仰，最后他告诉我，相机是被一个农民捡到的，他把相机交到了八达岭派出所。警察很清楚，这种相机是外国人丢的，后来他们通过机场海关，在我的申报单上查到是我的，最后通过旅行社很快送还给我。我太高兴了！到了 20 世纪 80 年代和 90 年代，随着去长城的游客蜂拥而至，我的柯尼卡相机再也没进过警察局，我只记得那些通过它的镜头拍下的许多照片。时至今日，这架柯尼卡相机连同莱卡相机一直默默地陪伴我周游列国。

相机失而复得，那时候的风气确是这样。又如，如果我在商店里付完钱，忘记拿找回的零钱就出门，商店的服务员会赶紧追出来，将发票、小票和零钱交给我，他们绝对不收小费。那时不许收小费，收小费甚至会被认为是不光彩的事。但是中国还能与世界隔绝多久？无论如何，一个如此伟大的和具有如此潜力的国家，怎么可能使它处于封闭状态？毛泽东大胆地试图"创造"乌托邦式的"新"人，他也这样做了。(20世纪) 80年代初期，有了一次相当规模的社会和政治的电休克，现在进行着一次真正的跃进，甚至一次翻跟斗的三级跳的时机已经成熟。所有的前提条件已经存在，私有化和集体的团结互助精神，无论怎样理解，都会产生它们的成果。作为改革家的邓小平重返舞台后，进行了另一种大胆的尝试，即"创建"带有明显儒家思想的社会主义市场经济。北京从"新"人的试验中走出来，站在了实现"四个现代化"试验的前列。我是这个号召解放思想和开放边界的历史性过渡的见证人。"又红又专"的口号被"不管白猫黑猫，抓到老鼠就是好猫"的口号所替代。审判"四人帮"之后，对过去做出的历史评价是：毛泽东是新中国的建筑师，功过为三七开："七分功劳，三分错误"。在经历文化革命的过分甚至狂热之后，中国承认需要再次返回"世界"，邓小平的中国创造了现代化的难以置信的奇迹。通过提出"从现在起到2000年，把中国建设成为一个富裕和现代化的国家"的口号，开始了可能持续一个世纪的史诗般周期才能完成的第二次大革命。毛泽东曾在20世纪50年代预言："毫无疑问，下一个世纪将是中国的世纪"。他的预言是对的。

1986年夏天，为了庆祝我到中国10周年，我决定携全家四人去中国。这次我们是坐西伯利亚快运火车去的，从莫斯科出发穿越欧亚大陆，一个星期后到达中国。我的两个女儿，一个14岁，一个11岁，正处在一个这类旅行最理想的年龄，尽管我的太太提出种种不赞成的理由，但最后还是同意了。我们抵达北京的时间是7月一个天气

马达罗的太太和女儿游览长城

十分闷热的上午，我们像跑马拉松似的到了终点。对于一个从未体验如此经历的人来说，很难想象出这趟旅行的艰辛：9,000公里的铁路线，7天7夜在火车上生活，吃饭，睡觉，等待，观景，所有的时间都在火车上度过。我们横穿过的那片辽阔领土，那时还是在苏联统治下的禁区和警察严格监控的地区。在苏联，同俄国共产主义的一些不合情理现象的撞击，对我们来说也有很大的"教育"价值。在莫斯科，我们要去莫斯科的Jaroslavskaja 火车站，在俄罗斯的一家名叫Inturist 的旅行社预订好出租车，带我们去那里，但是出租车却要把我们送到另一个名叫明斯克的火车站。这会导致我们赶不上每周一趟穿越西伯

利亚的火车,我们的旅行也会因签证过期而取消。幸好此前我已经问过何处才是穿越西伯利亚的火车站。当我发现司机走错路的时候,我把他的车钥匙拔了下来,冲着他喊"Jaroslavskaja"、"Jaroslavskaja",他才改变了行车路线。我们到了车站广场,卸下行李后又遇到了困难。那里有两个火车站,一个在前一个在后。我给搬运工几个卢布作为小费,他凭直觉,匆忙地把我们的行李用他的小推车推到了一个栅栏前。我们又给了警察一些小费,并且对他说:"西伯利亚—北京",我们才走进了该去的火车站,直奔站台,那辆直达北京的长长的列车已经停靠在那里。在预订的车厢里,两个检票员挡住了我们的路,他们检查完我们的车票后,粗鲁地告知,我们需要分开住宿:妻子和女儿们的卧铺在一个车厢,而我的卧铺则在相邻的另一个车厢。怎么可能会出现这种问题?我预订车票时明明要求预订位于同一包间、铺位号相连的卧铺。是铁路人员自己搞错了?但列车员却说他们没有做出变更的权线。火车马上就要开了,时不我待。我闯入预订好的房间,等待列车长的到来。在经过一段很长时间的交涉后,列车长终于同意让我们四个人住在一起了。穿越苏联西伯利亚时还算顺利,只是我们用完了当作小费的卢布。我们一直去餐车用餐,吃得很好。但是那些从东欧回国的中国剧团的演员们就没有那么走运了,他们每次要去餐车吃饭都被粗暴地拒绝,真不知道他们这一星期是怎么度过的。列车每次停靠的站台上,除了一些盒装的海产品外,没有任何东西可买,当地居民还时不时跑上餐车去买面包。

到了中国,一切都变了:在满洲里车站,到处是欢迎的彩旗,站台商店的货架上商品琳琅满目。北京以她广阔的郊野向我们问候。在北京,东便门周边都是拆迁工地。一眼望去,角楼酷像一艘停泊在一片低矮房屋顶上的帆船,这里将要变成建国门商务区。面对眼前不同文化的冲撞,我的家人惊呆了:北京和我们离威尼斯不远的省城差别是如此之大。我对北京已相当熟悉,但是北京对我的两个女儿来说,一切是那么新奇。不过,反差激起了她们的兴趣。她们很快学会了几句中文,学会了用筷子吃饭,并且将所见所闻写在日记里。对于她们来说,这仅仅是她们"了解中国"之旅的开始。

也就是那年夏天,我认识了陆辛,后来他成为我深入了解中国不可或缺的朋友。当时我有位意大利朋友,他是一个意大利高档餐饮集团的老板,打算在北京开设第一家意大利餐厅,委托我联络此事。后来他决定与北京国际饭店合资经营,当时陆辛代表中方合资伙伴工作,是正在建造的

陆辛和女儿陆佳

北京国际饭店的一位年轻经理。我们在全家访华宴会上有幸结识，他那开朗的性格和热情诚恳的态度马上吸引了我。他当时刚30岁出头，和一个外交官的女儿结了婚，他们有一个3岁的女儿，我们都称呼她鲁琪娅。他毕业于北京大学西语系西班牙语专业，但他对科技产品很感兴趣，像照相机，摄像机，和后来出现的手机，电脑，GPS之类的。他给我解释他的名字，当我得知"辛"字意味着"辛勤"时，我意识到我发现了一个非常特殊的人才。他比我年轻，我就叫他小陆。一切如愿以偿：我在理想的时间，在理想的地方，找到了理想的人才。就我而言，很难再遇到比他更合适的人选了。他直觉敏锐，总能迅速找到解决问题的办法；当中外双方合作发生分歧时，他能灵活协调，使问题迎刃而解。他善于思考，总想寻找最佳方案；他当机立断，从不教条；他心胸开阔，时刻准备着迎接任何人生的挑战。陆辛以前是、现在是、今后仍然是我在北京所有活动的"维吉尔"*。他是我在中国旅行的重要伙伴。坦率地说，如果没有他，我真不知道对中国能了解多少。我们俩几乎走遍整个中国：从遥远的新疆到黑龙江，从内蒙古到西藏，从甘肃到海南岛。但是我们最感兴趣和谈论最多的还是北京。北京永远充满了神奇。我非常珍惜我们的友谊，这种友谊是无价之宝，坚不可摧。

我们的许多亲朋好友都知道，小陆和我老马

---

* 古罗马诗人，但丁最崇拜的作家，在《神曲》中，后者称他为"老师"。虚构他解救了迷路的自己，并邀请自己周游地狱和天国。

（他给我起的尊称）是一对永不分离的左膀右臂。多年来的交往，我们创造出我们自己的语言：一门别人听不懂的语言，一门混合着汉语、意大利语、英语、西班牙语和威尼斯方言的奇妙语言。我们抓住头脑中最先闪出的单词迅速造句。这种独特的语言组合使我们能够快速地沟通，而且可以在任何时候使用，特别是在大脑记忆容易混乱的晚餐桌上。我们还有自己独特的发音，比如说英语时候，发音由我们掌握，我们可以使用意大利语的发音，或者使用相应的汉语拼音，没有人能懂得我们在说什么，但是我们却很快就能听懂对方。语言对于我们来说就像一把钥匙，它能打开一扇沟通的大门，因此我们不太在意发音和语法的错误，只要打开这个门，理解对方就行。这几年我们不断完善我们的语言，提炼精辟的词句，充实大脑的词汇库，使我们可以更准确理解对方表达的意思。现在只需要说出一个词，我们彼此就能心领神会；只要说一个句子，就可以描述对一个人的综合评价。

在我多年的漫长的中国之旅中，陆辛一直是我的不可替代的"大管家"，他就像电影助理导演一样，你需要一套独立战争时的军服吗？一把17世纪的西班牙安乐椅吗？一辆1910年产的汽车吗？一台军用电话吗？一台留声机、一个斗士的头盔、一张13世纪的羊皮纸吗？陆辛就是你要找的助手，你的"大管家"。真的，一直到今天，陆辛真让人难以置信，我想要在中国找的东西，他都能找到，包括找人。找人真难！这是在一个深刻变化中的首都，有的居民区一夜间在推土机和炸药声音中变了样，有的胡同瞬间变成一堆瓦砾，某个街名或地名迅速在地图上消失。陆辛居然在为数不多的胡同里找到了一位手工艺人。这位艺人花费了多年的心血，用细木和火柴棍制作出京城 16 座城门的模型和其他老北京古建的模型。后来陆辛在一旧楼区，又找到一位不太出名的普通画家，他在文化大革命中，凭着记忆，一笔一画地画出一幅 50 米长的老北京风情画。陆辛甚至帮助我找到了中国末代皇帝溥仪的遗孀，当时她独自住在北京一座很普通的楼房里。

从那时候起，我开始喜欢研究北京的古建筑，特别是 20 世纪 50 年代初至 60 年代时还保留着的老北京城墙和 16 座城门中的 14 座城门。这些城门多数在后来的年代里被拆除了，只有东便门角楼，不知道何种原因，奇迹般地毫发无损。好奇心驱使我开始寻找淹没在低矮平房中的老北京城墙遗址，这是从东便门到我住的新侨饭店前的崇文门的一段城墙。这次考察我不想麻烦陆辛，在我看来，在那个时代，让他陪我这个"外国人"去参观这肮脏杂乱的地方，或者对这些愚蠢和不负责的规划品头论足都不太合适。我决定独自前往。某日清晨，我带上照相机前往，在当地居民好奇目光的注视下，穿过低矮简陋的板房和脏乱的小巷，来到旧城墙跟前。惊奇地发现，北京的旧城墙体依然保留着，依着城墙搭建了许多丑陋的简易房，这些房子居然是用旧城墙砖盖建的。他们用古城墙砖来修建住房，从东便门起，一直延伸到崇文门，至少有 2 公里长。必须拆掉城墙旁搭建的各种违章建筑，清除城墙周边的楼房，

用那些曾被挪用盖房的城墙砖来修复明城墙，这样才有可能把北京这段有着数百年历史、人类伟大奇迹之一的雄伟城墙还给北京。我奋笔疾书，向北京市委阐述了自己的观点。时隔不久，被认作是不可能的事发生了：城墙边的平房、楼房被一一拆除，用近两百万块旧城砖复原了城墙的原貌。数百年的古槐树保住了，明城墙遗址公园建成了！数年后的今天，这里已经变成老年人休闲散步的好去处。

也就是从那个时候起，我的朋友陆辛也对老北京古建筑产生了极大的热情，他跟着我开始对老北京进行新的探索寻访。我们日复一日地去探寻在革命年代里被覆盖和淹没的古建筑。我决定撰写一本书，书名是：《北京，天国的首都》。在书中，我要根据史料和多年的研究，详细描绘出一张老北京地图，此书至今尚未写完。《北京月刊（Beijing This Month）》杂志的主编开了一个专栏，介绍我在北京城的发现。经验告诉我，了解北京的民俗最好的时机是中国的春节。陆辛和他的家人陪同我逛了不少庙会，在这里你可以参观到许多业经修复重新开放的寺庙，触摸到城市的心脏，观赏文艺表演，品尝小吃。新的城市越兴起，越使我怀念她的过去，怀念她作为古都的令人惊叹的特征，正如我说的那样，是怀念她的特征，而不是她的外貌。

北京经历了一场巨变，在 20 世纪 80 至 90 年代期间，我来北京将近上百次，亲历了这条巨龙蜕皮换鳞的过程。日复一日，北京绿树成荫的院落不见了，浪漫和休闲的气氛几乎已消失殆尽。

她成了一座21世纪的大都市。我每次来，都会觉得又少了些东西，包括幽雅宁静的四合院。这种心灵的创伤总有一天会演变成剧痛。因为很显然，老房子拆掉后，人们一旦醒悟过来，还得重建。这种现象在近几年屡见不鲜，如故宫周边和鼓楼附近的许多老房子、旧街道都在陆续恢复从前的面貌；在前门大街地区也完全按照20世纪初期的样子恢复重建，还开通了有轨电车；还有重建永定门，永定门是北京外城的南门，20世纪50年代被拆掉了，后来在21世纪初在原址上重建。现在还正在研究地安门的重建项目，地安门南边乱搭建的房屋已拆除，露出原来内城墙的紫红色墙皮和黄色琉璃瓦。我相信，北京人对这座历史悠久的老北京城的怀念是非常深厚的，他们渴望更多的，特别是有代表性的古建筑，再回到人们的生活中。但是，在实现现代化的初期，不仅是胡同里鞑靼式样的老房子被拆掉，连门前神圣的古槐树也被挖走了，一个富有诗意的老北京消失了，同时也带走了一个贫穷的北京。一个更加美好和更加现代的城市工程建设，当然需要做出牺牲。北京还有不少居住条件很差的住房，没有自来水，没有卫生间，没有下水道，电线老化，街道狭窄。总而言之，一切都有待改善和重建。

30年来，中国政府为了保证人民生存，采取了必要的措施，但人口成倍增加的问题也很突出。毛泽东提出"丰衣足食"的口号，首先解决了每个人的吃饭穿衣问题，哪怕有一碗米饭和一件哥萨克式的棉衣也好，起码不会像过去那样饿死人。1949年，中国许多地方遭灾，到处是贫穷与饥饿，

死亡人数成天文数字。现在人口增长的速度已放慢，这要归功于80年代改革者们控制人口增长率的明智政策。北京也要从这个规则出发，需要提高人民生活水平，控制人口增长速度，规划建设新型城市。改革包括建立新型住宅、道路、医院、学校和饭店。政府要改善交通设施，增加就业机会，使更多的人有工作，哪怕那是工资只有数十元的普通工作。我一次又一次来北京时，看到了这种真正的革命热情，北京改变了面貌，成为一个现代化的首都，豪华的酒店等待大批游客的到来。这个奔向21世纪的不可遏制的进程，造成了不少"地方色彩"的破坏，但实际上这是一些不适合居住的破旧房屋，可以理解，只有留恋于过去的老人们希望把它们保留下来。我也非常喜爱那些胡同和百年的老槐树，我的心情，常常处于矛盾中，但我知道，贫穷不是一个不可放弃的条件，它有一个忍受的限度，在超越这个限度时可以不惜任何代价，甚至包括承受不可避免的投机风险。北京发生着翻天覆地的变化，天际线上充满着巨大的吊车和摩天大楼，逐渐变得一切都不认识了，那是一片一望无际的工地，我在那里看到了未来和可能出现的未来。中国的现代化建设的浪潮，比一百次地震还要强烈。我穿过一片废墟，这里的工人们正在堆码一批熏黑的旧房梁和灰色的砖头，场面如同被轰炸后一样。那里的胡同在怀旧的伤感中消失了，替代她的是宽阔的街道、高架桥、塔楼和广场，形成一个高档小区。人们自己也在变，不仅是穿衣打扮变了，他们的生活习惯和举止也西方化了。说实话，我不知道他

们是否为此感到幸福，当然这是社会学家应当回答的问题，然而我在30年前认识的那些富有感情的、不知道姓名的人，今天再也遇不到了，可是他们将永远留在我的心里，留在我当时所拍的照片里，他们总是高兴地同意我给他们拍照，有时怀着惊奇的目光，有时摆出幸福的姿势，特别是老人和孩子们。

1988年秋，我结束朝鲜访问后又到了北京。北京的秋天阳光明媚，树叶开始变黄。有一天我和陆辛在离鼓楼不远的地方散步。这里的胡同群保存完好无损。我们走了一个多小时，在一条不太宽的胡同里，发现胡同的一边是矮墙围着的破旧的四合院，而胡同的另一边是高墙大院，被郁郁葱葱的古槐笼罩着。由于胡同窄小，我们看不到高墙里边的房屋。奇异的事情发生了，那高墙仿佛是透明的，我突然"看透"了墙那边的所有东西。我问陆辛是否知道这个院子，他摇摇头。我清楚地说出了那里面的一切：一个堆满奇石的大院，绿草如茵、林木葱葱的小山，灰瓦亭台楼阁，雕刻着蝙蝠图案的石栏。庭院中有一人工湖，湖中有一小亭子，一座精美的小木桥把它和地面连接起来。我给陆辛描述我在院里"看到"的一切，他听呆了。的确，我以前从来没有进过这个院子，这完全是一种奇妙的"幻觉"。陆辛说我们一定要进去看个究竟。仅有的一扇大铁门，用铁链和大锁紧锁着。不远处有个自行车修理铺，陆辛让我在原地等他，他先去了解一下情况。我再次注视着这座高墙，顿觉有一股力量要把我推进这个我已经"见到"过的院子里。我以前可从来没有过

这种感觉，我惊异不已。过了几分钟，陆辛回来了，和他一起过来的，还有一个老人。他们走到我的面前，要我再次描述一下我所"看见"的东西。陆辛给老人翻译。我说完后，老人的神情大变，激动地眨着那双小眼睛。原来老人是这个院子的看门人，他把门打开，让我们进去。我恍然感到我曾经来过此地，但事实是我从未来过。难以置信的是这里的一切，居然正和我"见到"和描述的一模一样，甚至栏杆上的蝙蝠图案也那么相似。庭院里的许多建筑已年久失修，瓦片从房顶滑落到石子铺的小路上。唯一使我感到欣慰的是，这里的一切完好如初，没有遭到破坏。老人告诉我，这是那个倒霉的咸丰皇帝的弟弟恭亲王的府第，他死于1898年。说真的，我不知道这个人物，那时的北京地图上也没有标注这个古建筑。和老人道别后，陆辛反复地对我说，这件事实在不可思议。现在我并不想坚持这个故事，但是我只想补充说在此后的年代里，出现了一种与这个故事有关的奇怪。神秘的关系，经过13年徒劳的寻找之后，我终于以不同寻常的方式找到了1900年义和团运动时期意大利驻北京的公使朱塞佩·萨尔瓦戈·拉吉（Giuseppe Salvago Raggi）侯爵的外交皮箱。我翻阅那些文件，力图重新构建那次事件的历史，当我得到这只著名的皮箱时，我便联想起13年前我在北京发生的神秘事情，联系到在蒙费拉托山（公使的家乡）找到的那只皮箱。实际上在我找到的许多被保存下来的重要东西中，还有一本那位公使的珍贵日记，我从上面读到恭亲王曾经到意大利公使馆拜访过他，他也表示将

去回访恭亲王，可是数月后恭亲王突然去世。这两个事件——我的"幻觉"和找到的外交皮箱——经常被一种神秘的花的香味不可思议地联系在一起，可是当一切都以超现实的，甚至可以说是以难以理解的方式实现之后，这种花的香味就消失了。我想其中也许存在着奥妙，特别是我曾在不同的时间感觉到了那种香味，我在家中，在意大利时都闻到了那种香味，那是北京槐树花的香味，也就是恭王府花园里树梢晃动着的槐树花的花香，恭王府是在现代化城市包围中的一座过去的孤岛。

20世纪结束之前和1997年香港回归中国之后，我更加紧了对古老北京的研究，因为我感觉到这个城市正在丧失旧有的神韵，这点曾被20世纪初的西方旅行家视为混乱，毫无逻辑、难以理解。而我的看法却正好相反，我认为北京是一座"理想的城市"，它是根据复杂的道家风水学说，按照起源于某种占卜术的几何学原理修建的。我认为北京像一个隐秘的女儿，我必须要解开她的秘密，认识她。我最感兴趣的是我要研究何处是北京与西方的破裂点，由此产生北京与西方之间如此的不理解和不信任。我相信1900年夏天发生的义和团运动，在此之前就有一系列无休止地敌视中国的行动，之后的残酷镇压又导致北京蒙受被烧杀抢掠和宏伟建筑遭到毁坏的耻辱，这就是同西方发生悲剧性破裂的基础。我不相信我在阅读某些历史学家或伪历史学家在他们的著作中对这场悲剧事件所作的介绍，他们都毫无例外地按照反对印第安人的西部电影中表现的那样，结束时都是"我们的人"到达后取得了胜利。我在英国作家P.弗莱明（Peter Fleming）的一本书中读到，意大利公使萨尔瓦戈·拉吉"是在公使馆区内唯一继续着装赴宴的人"，这是唯一慷慨提到我们外交代表的一句话。我开始寻找那些肯定保存在某个档案室或某个偏僻阁楼上的文件。那句有点半开玩笑的话，提示我注意到那位"继续着装赴宴"的公使不仅是一位真正的绅士，而且是一位拘泥于细节的人。因此，我开始翻阅他的文件，他用打字机写的公文副本，也许还有他的笔记，这些东西可能让我重新写一段有关北京的重要历史。在外交文件箱中，实际上我找到了与事情的发展有些不一样的证据，把我引向恭亲王的神秘线索，与其说是偶然机会，还不如说是命中安排。

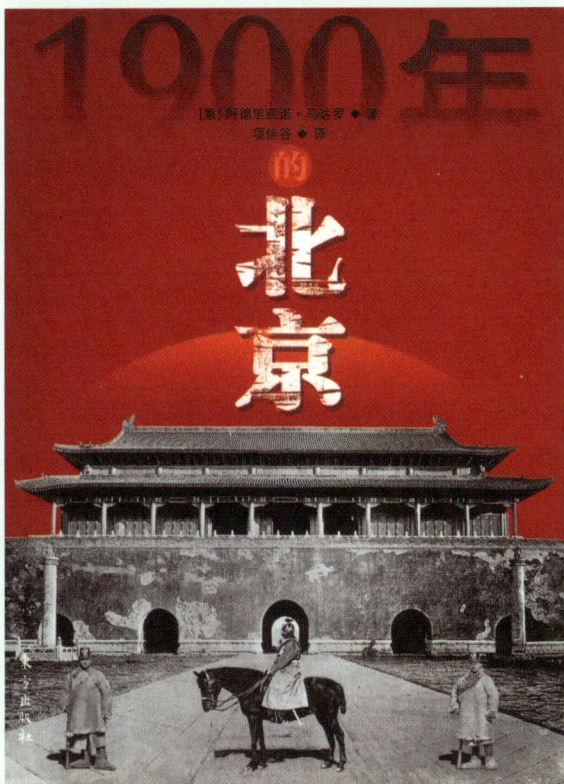

那个产生"幻觉"的奇妙的下午，以它那闪烁着金黄色树叶的景色铭刻在我的心里。那天夜里突然从蒙古刮来的强风，猛烈地撞击在我房间窗户的玻璃上，发出魔鬼般的叫声，仿佛是一群无限哀伤的地狱里的幽灵在呻吟。我无法入睡，聆听幽灵们的诉说，它们的凄凉的呼叫声包含着无限的痛苦。我总把北京想成是一个巨大的精神聚会的桌子，在狂风之夜，一代一代的幽灵们在这里聚会，他们惊愕地看到他们的世界发生了怎样翻天覆地的变化。也许恭亲王就在他们中间。第二天早上，冬天来了。光秃秃的树枝伸向青灰色的天空，所有的树叶都躺在了地上，清洁工们将它们扫成一个个巨大的黄叶堆。在北京就是这样，一夜大风之后，冬天就来临了，寒风吹落了所有槐树的树叶，完全改变了前一天还是温暖的秋日景色。

新世纪初，北京的深刻变化中添加了"美国的"特色。麦当劳和肯德基连锁店的快速增长像吸铁石一样吸引着年轻人。我惊奇地看到，与这些西方快餐（官方并不是很欢迎）一起的，还有完全不同于中国传统饮食的牛奶，也在迅速普及。以前总是说，中国人大多缺少帮助消化乳糖的必需的酶，但是随着新世纪的到来，新一代人的饮食和口味也发生了迅速的变化。开始是在三里屯的使馆区，接着在"后海"的沿湖一带，后来在面积相当大的朝阳区，都大量出现了酒吧和夜总会，爵士和摇滚乐队的声音响彻通宵，含酒精的饮料被畅饮如河。出现了大排量的外国品牌的轿车，精美的豪华卫生间，对财富的炫耀，东方的

享乐主义比西方的更粗俗、更奔放，也比西方的更引人注目。

许多来自欠发达的省份以及尚处于贫困地区的年轻人，受电视广告的影响来到北京，这些电视广告向他们炫耀首都的繁华和大批的就业机会。打工族们，远离自己出生和成长的老家，闯荡在一个从未居住过的陌生的城市。北京人好像并不欢迎这些自由的冒险家们，因为他们的到来增加了社会压力，北京人抱怨这些寻求好运的淘金者的涌入，打乱了这座大城市的宁静，改变和弱化了老北京的特色。社会的环境在飞快地改变，一方面，北京人留恋着将被现代化所取代的老北京城风貌，留恋着他们所创造的带有"儿化"音的老北京方言，他们喜爱听京剧，至今仍保持着北京人特有的"天子脚下爷儿们"的豪气；另一方面，新来的移民，他们看不起靠着首都吃皇粮的寄生方式，他们在奋力寻求自己的机遇，为了站住脚，他们不在乎从事何种职业。还有外国人，就像蜜蜂喜欢蜂蜜一样从地球的各个角落纷至沓来，他们想在这里打造一个与他们本土生活相似、与社会隔绝的、属于他们自己的私密空间和生活方式，他们的外国护照和鼓鼓囊囊的钱包则是他们的保护伞。只有极少数外国人，他们是真正的"中国通发烧友"，他们试图融入到普通的首都居民生活中去，表示他们已经"入乡随俗"，但是这些人为数极少。更多的外国人，或者说绝大多数的外国人，都在这里辛勤地加速建设着自己的"小世界"，他们的心目中充满了无限的优越感。北京乃至中国，正在经历着一场蜕变，这些美丽的蝴蝶

破茧而出，产生了令人敬畏的不可抑制的力量。

西方至今还不甚了解中国发生了巨大的变化。我从三十多年的中国经历得出一个看法：从1976年春季的第一次至2008年秋季的最近一次去中国，时间的跨度无法比拟。这是一场根本性的变革，"中国精神"真是神秘莫测，悠远过去和刚渐逝的过去是紧密衔接的。如果你认为，北京在某月某日将会变成西方的一座现代化大都市，那你就错了。恰恰相反，北京是一座亚洲人的最重要的城市之一，是亚洲所期望、真心诚意期望的城市缩影，是一座新的现代化和不同文明交相辉映的典范城市；如果你认为，北京是中国西方化的前哨，那你又错了。相反，北京总有一天会领导和带动世界变化的潮流，就像今天带动中国的变化一样。中国人的改革成功，其原因是因为他们始终坚持不懈地在探索着适合本国国情的改革模式，这一崇高的美德，我们西方人必须认识到。飞速的发展使中国重新坐回了她在1839年前坐过的、后来被外国入侵者发动殖民战争夺走的位置，回到了世界级大国的地位上。在19世纪中叶前的数千年里，中国一直是世界经济与文化的强国，而今天，中国还依旧是政治与军事的强国。

思想理论家毛泽东曾预言"东风压倒西风"，当时他坚定地认为中国革命会战胜西方的反攻。但是由于毛泽东，是位道家哲学的学者，认同对立统一的学说，所以他这句话很可能寓意着中国的未来将立于世界之林，他提到的西方，是指全世界。

我很自然地接受了他的这种理论，因为我亲身体会到了30年"翻天覆地"的变化，再一次感受到毛泽东预言的意义。现在中国在腾飞，势不可挡，绝对没有驻足的理由。一个很有意思的问题是：必须充分认识这场伟大变革所带来和继续带来的影响，这种影响不仅涉及到中国人的生活方式，还会涉及到他们的古老文化，关系到中国自孔子以来七十多代人的遗传基因，这些人的"人生观"在发展上不同于我们西方。北京是我们了解中国的标尺，不过对我们西方人来说，其检测标准是难以掌握的，很容易造成混乱。我们的理解也经常是错误的：用我们西方人的观点看问题，往往把事情看得简单化。

但是，如果仔细观察北京这座伟大的城市，我们不难发现，北京人的生活习惯依然没有太大的改变：舞台变了，银幕上高楼林立，一派现代建筑群的新貌，而北京人生活习性没有变。在日坛公园，你仍然可以买到小金鱼，可以看到手里拎着竹编的鸟笼遛鸟的老人。老北京人至今还保留的任何生活细节，决不会逃过我这双训练有素的神眼，传统的生活方式仍在延续。节假日期间，如果你从天坛公园东门进去，你会看到唱京戏和演奏乐器的仍然聚会在露天场所，在他们的周围，围满了他们的"粉丝"和京剧迷；在另一地方，一排排的歌咏队，像教堂的唱诗班那样有节奏地唱着怀旧的革命歌曲；在地坛公园，仍然有斗蟋蟀的场所，葫芦罐里的蟋蟀，在它们主人手中小棍的挑动下，不时发出阵阵和谐的叫声。在天安门广场上，五花八门的风筝仍在翱翔，觅食的老鹰，大尾巴摇摇摆摆的金鱼，在天空舞动的长龙。在北京,任何有风的日子都会看到这些风筝竞技者。这是 1978 年还是 2008 年?这个问题重要吗?北京还是北京,依然如故。

　　盛况空前的北京2008年奥运会,让我再次见证了北京乃至全中国发生的巨变,对于我来说,新建的首都国际机场与1976年我第一次踏上中国国土时让我晕头转向的那个老机场相比,简直天壤之别,我好像来到一个新的星球上一样。北京和中国发生如此翻天覆地的变化令人惊叹不已,这在我来中国旅行的最初几年里,简直想都不敢想。飞机在新机场降落时,我注意到首次来中国的外国游客下机后那惊呆的神态,我不知道在他们来华之前,了解到多少关于这个伟大国家的现代化进程,但是眼前的现实,足以震撼着他们。而我,在 32 年内 155 次对这个国家的不同访问后,我可以自豪地说,我是这个国家30年来变化的每一个阶段见证人。可是当我见到了新机场以后,这个代表整个中国的现代化的新建筑形象又让我吃惊了。世界上没有任何一座机场可以和这座机场相媲美,世界上不可能有任何城市,像北京那样提供现代的和有效、完美的配套设施:高速公路、高架桥、摩天大楼、酒店、购物中心和住宅小区。在当今世界,北京和现代化是同义词,这座辉煌的首都已成为有成就的、备受世界关注的城市典范。

　　2008年的奥运会给了中国一个展示自己的机会,它告诉了世界,中国是认真的:比赛平稳地在安全和有效气氛中进行。北京的各项工作向世界交了一份满意的答卷。她可以无愧地进入国际城市的前列。当我看到所有这一切,总是拿她和30 年前所见到的相比,回味 30 年来与中国人民建立的友谊,与北京这座大城市千丝万缕的联系,"我的"北京,是星球上最迷人的目的地之一:因为1976年是一个封闭、神秘、陌生的北京,而2008年是一个开放、透明、现代化的北京。伟大的长城不再是"隔断",她是"纽带"的象征,是把中国和世界紧紧联在一起的纽带。

陆辛　翻译

An Eye-witness In Beijing

It wasn't possible to get to Beijing. It was already eight o'clock in the evening, too late. The weekly flight from Paris, passing over Italy, Albania, Persia, Pakistan and the Himalayas, before entering Xinjiang in China, had landed almost an hour late. During the long approach and landing, not a single light was visible, and I felt that I had arrived in one of the remotest corners of the world. As I came down the steps and walked across the tarmac, my first impression of China was a waft of kerosene, and the first image an enormous picture of Mao, weakly floodlit, on the front of the airport building. Above me, there was a starry sky that I was rarely to see again in Beijing.

I had flown for almost twenty hours, with a single stop in Karachi, in a Boeing 707 of the Chinese state airline packed with disciplined little men all dressed in blue and black jackets and peaked caps. The women, dressed the same, were hardly distinguishable.

The airport lounge, where two young hostesses in light blue tunics and slippers invited me to sit, was filled with an intense perfume of jasmine. The huge armchairs, upholstered in deeply worn leather, were each covered with an embroidered cloth, carefully indicating their hierarchical importance. It was a VIP lounge with two large pictures filled with complex, decorative ideograms, and on the low table, where large teacups were ranged around an enormous red-enamelled thermos, a single lilac branch rose from a glass vase. That small touch of gentility, showing none of the revolutionary fervour of those years, was an ideogram which I took instantly as a good augury. The two hostesses returned with sad expressions and told me in barely comprehensible English that I would not be able to get into the city that night, it was too late, there were no taxis and nobody would be able to take me until the following morning. So they escorted me into the dining room for dinner. I knew nothing of my luggage; we had not gone through a reclaim area as none existed. But I was no more worried about my bags than I was about how or where I was to spend the night.

It was the evening of April 29th 1976, and after a wait of many years and an interminable flight, I had arrived in the heart of the mysterious and "forbidden" China, still shrouded in the myth of the Maoist revolution. The excitement of my awareness that I had finally reached the forbidden country allowed me no other thoughts, and I surrendered myself to the surroundings of my first hours in China. The odour, the atmosphere and the feel of the Cultural Revolution hung in the air like the smell of the kerosene and the jasmine, and, if truth be told, the stench of garlic which swept over me with every breath of the young hostesses whose movements I followed as I gazed at the napes of their necks framed by two thick, swinging plaits of black hair.

The dining room of the airport had two large, round tables. Along the wall, ten waitresses in white coats were lined up, arms hanging at their sides, and they rushed as one to the table laid for ten where I had been asked to sit. I looked around curiously, but saw no other guests, and was amused to find myself surrounded by a gaggle of young girls, all anxious to serve me; a situation hardly revolutionary but very comforting for a guest who had come so far. I understood nothing of their Chinese, and the two hostesses were unable to translate, and so they began to bring from the kitchen an extraordinary number dishes; an abundance of food that led me to think that they I would be enjoying the company of ten fellow diners. How was I to eat ten fried eggs, or finish off three enormous plates of meat, three of fish and three of vegetables, as well as a bowl of rice and a small mountain of steam-cooked bread? The ten beers were also somewhat in excess of requirements, and I laughed when my ten guardian angels, disappointed at my meagre appetite, had to take away almost the entire banquet.

When I finished dinner, the two hostesses returned to take me somewhere I could sleep, but I said it was too early, and that I wanted to see the airport. Amazed by my request at such a late hour (nine o'clock), they indicated that I should follow them. In the main lounge, the shift workers, all apparently teenagers, were involved in a revolutionary committee meeting. They sat cross-legged on the ground, with the famous little red book in their hands, engaged in heated discussion. A great statue of Mao surrounded by vases of flowers dominated the room.

I asked what they were talking about so animatedly, and one of them, who spoke some English, told me they had to decide who would have responsibility for the airport on the following day. Was this a good time to ask what had happened to my luggage? Could I make such a futile, egoistic-bourgeois request in the middle of a revolutionary discussion about a strategic decision amongst the proletarian collective of the airport of the Chinese capital?

I crossed the esplanade in front of the building from where an avenue lined with poplar trees led to Beijing, and entered the barracks on the right. I found a soldier at attention standing guard over my luggage. At the door of the barracks, which was to be my hotel for the night, my two hostesses bade me good night with a bow, by no means servile but very courteous, and told me that at seven o'clock someone would wake me and take me back to the dining room for breakfast. And Beijing? Later. After breakfast someone else would come to take me into the city. The little room in which I was promptly locked as soon as I had stowed away my bags. The two iron beds were immediately reminiscent of an old hospital, but were brightened up by pink and blue embroidered quilts. On the little wooden table, stood the usual set of covered tea cups and a thermos of boiling water. Two small armchairs with embroidered white covers and a three-legged wooden coat-stand completed the furnishings. A small iron door led to the squalid little squatting toilet. The window was barred as in a cell, and the light curtain embroidered with peonies. I realised immediately that at five o'clock the sun would come streaming in and I would be woken up, and as it was now almost ten, i.e. the middle of the night, I climbed into the nearest bed and fell fast asleep. I slept magnificently that first night in China; a deep sleep that I hadn't experienced for years, and who knows how long it would have lasted if I hadn't been woken by the imperious sound of a bugle immediately followed by the screeching of a loudspeaker. I jumped out of bed and pulled back the curtain bright with sunlight. My eyes fell on an army in underpants, haphazardly lined up, performing rhythmic gymnastics, while an officer perched on a trestle called out the rhythm, "Yi, Er, San. Yi, Er, San. One, Two, Three.", alternating with the shouted slogans which were more familiar in the China of the time: "Mao Zhuxì Wansuì!" Ten thousand years to Chairman Mao!

The little man in the blue jacket tightly buttoned up to his chin, and the shiny black fountain pen in his breast pocket, greeted me with a breezy "Bonjour monsieur", laughing through his somewhat irregular teeth. His hair, in serious need of the attentions of a brush, and eyes puffy with sleep were the two things which struck me about the young interpreter, providentially assigned to me by the State Tourist Agency. He presented himself without further ado; he was Comrade Fan Chuan-sheng, at my disposal to make my stay in Beijing as pleasant as possible, and to inform me, firmly but courteously, about what I could do and about what, out of respect for the laws of the People's Republic of China, I should not do. I was immediately taken by his air of sad awareness of all the courteous refusals that he would have to make. How was I going to get him on my side, and turn him into a precious ally in making my first steps to understand his country? He looked at me with sudden friendliness, and told me that the hotel to which I had been assigned was called the Hsin Chiao (today, in Pinyin, Xin Qiao), and that even though it had been built with the help of the Russians, it was very comfortable and was right in the centre of the city. He scrupulously avoided, however, telling me that it was at the beginning of what had been the Legation Quarter at the time of the Boxer Rebellion. He told me also that it had, on its third floor, the only western restaurant in Beijing, but that this was only open for breakfast, adding that he would provide me with any other information as and when it was necessary, and assuring me that he would follow me like my shadow, and that any idea of free movement was out of the question. As if he and I were old friends, he introduced me to our driver, who replied with a polite "ni hao", words which immediately entered my new vocabulary.

The road for Beijing was little more than an asphalted country lane, with double rows of poplars forming a green tunnel, down which advanced with exasperating slowness a procession of carts, trucks, coaches and the occasional car, accompanied by swarms of dour cyclists slowly pedalling forwards. At every crossroads, it seemed inevitable that the bedlam of movement would tangle itself into countless accidents which were, somehow, miraculously averted without even provoking a reaction. Then, as the mass moved forward once more, slowly extricating and disentangling itself, each person headed for his destination through the clouds of cotton-wool from the poplar trees, which swirled thickly in the air. The surrounding land was worked intensively, and looked like a gigantic kitchen garden, but I couldn't see a single house or village, just groups of peasants bent over, scratching at the yellow, dusty earth around a red flag blowing gaily in the breeze. The outskirts of Beijing appeared as small, clay-built houses with curved, grey roofs and shabby, jerry-built apartment blocks in ugly bare concrete. The surrounding greenery mitigated the otherwise disquieting vista of groups of small grey houses standing in the shadow of great acacia trees. The previously overwhelming sense of the countryside removed all sense of perspective: I had entered the mystery of Beijing without even being aware of it. The further I went, the more the trees dominated the houses, allowing me only glimpses of the grey walls and lacquered doors with their jaunty little roofs. There were crowds everywhere, and the streets bustled with life and activity, as if the people lived in the streets and the little houses were merely a backdrop to the great parade of life rather than the dwellings of the participants. I did not realise that those endless suburbs of bicycles, handcarts, horse-drawn wagons, noisy trucks, overcrowded buses, pedestrians, and townspeople standing at their doors waiting for someone or gazing at the passers-by, I did not realise that all that was in itself Beijing. I was crossing it and it felt like everything and anything but a city. Its dusty, rustic appearance, the simplicity of the buildings, the tangled mass of humanity dressed in blue cotton, the absence of solemn buildings and streets, the quiet continuity of the acacias whose light foliage covered and partly hid almost everything, all suggested the edge of a town bordering on the countryside, not the pulsating heart of a capital, the capital of China. The endless, teeming suburbs suggested nothing of military pomp or the solemnity of a regime. The capital of Red China had greeted me with disarming and benevolent humanity, surprising me with its relaxed normality. We entered a wide avenue and my friend Fan promptly informed me that it was the legendary Chang'an, Perpetual Peace, which led to Tian'anmen Square. The road was lined with the usual small, grey houses overhung by acacias; only the traffic was a little more urban, and we turned into Wangfujing Street, the most important shopping street in the city, dominated by the enormous Beijing Hotel. Finally, I saw more significant buildings, the crowds jostled along the tree-lined pavements and the shops thronged with customers. We drove past a

church surrounded by a solid wall, it was the Cathedral of the East, and a little further on, within sight of the yellow roofs of the Modern Art Gallery, we stopped in front of a three-sided building clearly of Soviet construction, the ugly style of the 1950s which had spread right across Eastern Europe. It was the hotel reserved for Chinese living abroad, the Hua Chiao. I got out here as the building contained the office where my passport had to be checked; in fact, no one had asked me for it at the airport the previous evening. As I got out of the car, I breathed in for the first time the smell of fried rice. I entered the bare lobby and Fan pointed me towards the door of the visa office. We were offered a cup of tea, and the formalities were dealt with very quickly. Fan said something which brought out a hearty laugh from the official, who handed me my passport with both hands, a custom which the Chinese maintain today when presenting business cards. Everything was fine, I was now officially registered, we could now go to my hotel. Thirty-two years later, I think back to the first steps I took in Beijing in that lobby. In the late 1990s, the hotel was renovated, enlarged and modernised to become a prestigious five-star establishment, and was to become my permanent "home" in Beijing under the name Hua Qiao Da Sha.

The Hsin Chiao, however, was not far from the station, just outside the Chongwenmen Gate, which had been knocked down in 1969. My room faced south, towards the "Chinese city", and I pondered on the reputation that the hotel had. It had been the hotel of Edgar Snow, the famous American journalist and author of Red Star Over China, who in the 1930s had had the courage to cross the Nationalist lines of Chiang Kai-shek in order to visit Mao and the Red Army in the revolutionary base of Yan'an. In the 1960s and 70s, he had returned to China as Mao's guest and had stayed here. Throughout the Cultural Revolution, the Hsin Chiao had been used by delegations from countries that were "friends of the revolution", and the staff were well trained in dealing with "barbaric" guests whose bizarre tastes and habits included the use of knives and forks, the need to have shirts and trousers ironed, and the use of the telegraph given that telephone connections were still difficult. As soon as I had settled into my room, to which I had been given a heavy brass key attached to a large aluminium fob bearing in red the four ideograms of the hotel, "Hsin Chiao hotel", the everfriendly Fan took me to the post office in a corner of the lobby, where I wrote out in block letters a telegram to be sent home: "Arrived Beijing OK beautiful sunshine". In the evening, I insisted on making a phone call and as there were no phones in the rooms I had to book the call with the attendant on my floor, who stood at the counter at the end of the corridor equipped with a thermos and a phone. With my passport in my hand, I had to fill in a form and then wait almost the whole night for the boy to come and knock on my door as one could only get through to

Italy after making interminable link-ups via Siberia. At that time, a future of mobile phones was unimaginable, or even the idea of lying comfortably in bed and making a call with the bedside phone. It was all down to the innocence of Fan, who one day much later was to come to Italy as a guest in my house, that I was able to enter into the everyday spirit of Beijing so quickly.

While I had agreed with him a programme to visit the unmissable sights, unbeknownst to my new friend, whose main concern was that I was ready at eight o'clock when the driver arrived, I had also worked out for myself an entirely different, unofficial programme. In Beijing, after dinner finished at about half past seven, the evening stretched ahead like a desert. There was almost no one in the streets, the restaurants, cinemas and theatres were closed by eight, the taxis no longer ran, and the hotel rooms had no televisions. The depressing experience of walking in the streets meant that one might, at most, come across the odd horse-drawn cart coming from the country, loaded with vegetables for a morning market. So I was often in bed by nine, and when dawn broke I got up, often before five, washed hurriedly in cold water, as there was no hot, shaved using water from the thermos, dressed and went out with my inseparable Leica round my neck. The night porter looked at me in some surprise at the early hour, but greeted me courteously with a bright "ni hao!".

An old map from Imperial times was etched on

my mind. The geography of Beijing had not changed all that much since then. Apart from the outrageous destruction of the Tartar walls and almost all of the old city gates, the city had remained essentially unchanged and all the major buildings were still in place. Many temples had been turned into schools, or factories, or warehouses but they were still there in the places I had memorised. But above all it was the essential fabric of the Beijing of the people, the tangle of innumerable hutung, the warren of streets and alleyways and lanes, the tight network of the "Tartar city" and of the "Chinese city", that had remained almost intact. Every morning, during my first visits to the city in the latter half of the 1970s, I set out on my solitary wanderings through the heart of the real Beijing; the unknown city, now becoming so familiar, thus revealed itself to me with disarming sincerity. I was quite alone but never felt that I was, as I was surrounded by the courtesy of people who were amused by my photographic acrobatics, and did not feel violated by the "foreign" eye of my camera. The more immersed I became in daily life, the more I felt immersed in good feeling, and even in poverty there was always great dignity. The children on their way to school, with their folding chairs because the schools were too poor to provide them, the old men peacefully smoking their long pipes, the women engaged in all their timeless occupations, the street traders with their infinity of wares to be bought or sold, the shopkeepers who invited me into their poky little rooms,

the house owners with their friendly gestures who invited me to enter the little courtyard of a siheyuan-the typical square houses of Beijing to offer me a cup of tea or some toasted sunflower seeds. I derived the profoundest pleasure from wandering through the shadowy warren of hutung, when Beijing was nothing but a complex of hutung, with no aim but to drink in with my eyes and my heart the humanity offered by those people, never hostile, always smiling; even the last Red Guards, proud of their armbands, no longer authoritarian, but still symbols of a patriotism that I could all too easily understand. During that distant spring, Mao was still alive and his overarching presence could be felt everywhere, as if his charisma had reached a state of beatification, and he had already been transformed into a divinity. His good-natured features adorned not only the palaces of Tian'anmen Square, but all public buildings, ever vigilant, more reassuring than fear-inspiring.

Pinyin, the transliteration of ideograms with the romanisation of sounds, had yet to be introduced, so that the names of streets and hutung, and any other signs were all in Chinese characters which I was beginning to understand and recognise. One of the first things I learnt was the points of the compass, of which there are five in China not four, as apart from north, south, east and west, there is also the centre, zhong, which is the most important and indicates, for example, Tian'anmen, the heart of Beijing. To find my way around, I never asked whether I should turn right or left, but towards the north or the south, asking where zhong was, as my hotel was not far from Tian'anmen. Looking at the street signs, which still today tell you whether you are north, south, east or west relative to the centre, finding my way was easy, as when I was in the "Internal Southern Street" of Andingmen, to get home I had to get to the "Internal Northern Street" of Chongwenmen, as my hotel was at the crossroads with the "Internal Western Street" of Dongbianmen. I often engaged in an entertaining exercise in orientation: by observing the position of the sun, and identifying the high, yellow roofs of the Forbidden City amongst the grey roofs of the rest of Beijing, I soon found my way. It seems impossible today but at that time there were very few buildings taller than the Hall of Supreme Harmony, and from the right angle, I was always able to see the yellow roofs sticking up above the trees. They were my reference point and at dusk they shone brightly in the gloom like fried eggs in a great bowl of spinach.

Life was slow, like that in a country village, and followed the pace of the bicycles which at certain times of the morning and afternoon swarmed along the streets to the tinkling of innumerable bells. In the early morning one could see older people performing the harmonious movements of Taiji in gardens and open spaces along the streets, or others twirling wooden swords decorated with red silk bows, and younger people performing gymnastics to mournful, martial music, their faces thrust forward as if chal-

lenging an imaginary enemy. There were few taxis, and they never stopped in the street; to get one, you had to go to one of the mere handful of hotels which existed in those days where they began and ended their journeys. One was advised to eat in the hotels as the food was more "international", in the sense that one could choose Cantonese or Sichuanese dishes, better known to foreigners, and regarded as somewhat exotic by the people of Beijing. One of my favourite restaurants was a large Islamic establishment at the Xidan crossroads, frequented by intellectuals from the nearby bookshop. I was always greeted with great kindness and offered a seat on the upper floor where tablecloths were provided, and the beer was kept in the fridge; a special concession for foreigners, as the Chinese would never dream of drinking anything cold, but would always drink hot water even at the height of summer, perhaps with a pinch of salt.

In the semi-deserted courtyards of the Forbidden City, the visitors gazed in astonishment at their surroundings, and with their peasants' hands caressed the gilded lacquer and the sculptures which adorn the Celestial Palace. The people, dressed in cotton, wandered as if in a dream where the silk-clad feet of the Emperors had trod, amazed by the abundance of beauty. Their eyes fell uneasily on the throne of Heaven, the symbol of the sacred power they had overthrown; they now stood in awe, tremulous at having dared to do so much. Their yearning for the sacred was palpable, and a slow caressing music descended from the great curved roofs, down the marble steps, spread into the corners of the great courtyards, and died away in the shadow of the dragons grinding the teeth of their great maws. I watched those poor peasants as they wandered with respect through that supremely beautiful place which to my eyes too seemed of such perfection as to transport the soul. With the enthusiasm of the newcomer, I pointed my lens at everything, as the good Fan regarded me with a mixture of scepticism and amusement for the way in which the remote past of the Forbidden City had so touched my soul. I explained to him that the ancient builders had created a perfect harmony, and that for me this place represented the quintessence of ancient Chinese civilisation. He laughed with great understanding for my exaggerated praise for a past which he himself criticised, but admitted that a degree of revision was necessary. To discredit the "feudal" past was a natural political position at the time, but the relaxation which had followed the excesses of the Cultural Revolution, and accompanied the slow demise of Chairman Mao, was already in the air. I felt the sense of anticipation one has as a great event approaches, the anxious trepidation that something is about to happen, but has not yet happened. In the spring of 1976, five months before the death of the Great Helmsman, Beijing was living in the drugged atmosphere of a painless illness.

A trip to the Great Wall took me into the depths of the countryside. The ancient road climbed up the sides of windswept mountains. We went through villages straight out of the tales of Lu Xun, with flocks of sheep and goats perched on the rocks in search of a few blades of grass. At Badaling, the tourists were the same curious peasants. The sight of a "waiguoren", i.e. a foreigner, aroused timorous curiosity. They were peasants on a trip from some distant corner of this immense country, and had brought with them enormous supplies of food and their beautiful children all wrapped up in coloured quilts. The Wall was breathtaking in its massive solidity. It was there, beneath my feet and before my eyes, running right across the horizon, springing across the valleys and bounding up the hillsides: a symbol of the tenacity of these people and of their will to survive in peace. "If we do not reach the Great Wall, we are not real Chinese", Chairman Mao had written in a famous poem at the time of the Long March. There was an incontestable truth in that phrase, the awareness of belonging to a great country which the Wall represented. In the following years, when the country had opened up to international tourism, my trips to the Wall confirmed the debasement of the myth and an almost "spiritual" decline. With the arrival of the seething crowds of package tour holidaymakers, Badaling became a kind of caravanserai of sellers of tasteless tourist tat. This was, of course, another sign of the new openness, but I felt great nostalgia for the days of the peasants who had travelled to the Wall in the spirit of the Long March. The first images that I had captured there alone, a few years before, remained more vivid in my heart than they could ever be on photographic paper. And it was the same for all the other places I visited, from the Temple of Heaven to the Summer Palace, where I met the people of Beijing who influenced me so much in my future understanding. It wasn't the local colour which struck me as much as the honest simplicity of an uncorrupted people who were happy to welcome the stranger from the distant West.

During my second trip, in 1977, I left one of my two cameras on a terrace on the Wall. I only realised when were almost back in the city, and Fan gave me a thorough dressing down for my forgetfulness. On the following afternoon, when I came back from a visit to the Fragrant Hills, I opened my door and was amazed to discover the Konica that I had "lost" on the Great Wall standing on my desk alongside a note written in English: "Kind friend, we ask you not to forget your things, or, if it happens, to remember where you left them so that they can be returned to you. It would be regrettable if you went home without your things". I was astounded. Where on earth could anything similar have happened? What kind of country was China that it could teach me such a lesson? The next day I told Fan what had happened, and asked him how the camera had been found, and how they knew it was

mine so that it could be given back. He chuckled at my ingenuous amazement, and explained that a peasant had found it and handed it in to the police post in Badaling. As it clearly belonged to a foreigner, they had traced me through the customs declaration I had made at the airport, and through the Tourist Agency they had quickly got back to me. Happy? In the 1980s and 90s, with the ravening hordes of tourists who swarmed over the Wall, my Konica would never have made it to a police post, and I would only have remembered it through the photographs taken through its lens. As it is, I still have it, along with my Leica, mute testament to my distant journeys.

But in those days it was like that. If I forgot even the smallest amounts of change in a shop, the shop assistant would run after me in the street with the fapiao, the receipt, and with the change, which he would categorically refuse to accept as a tip. Tips were, in fact, indecorous, almost offensive. But for how much longer could China remain cut off from the rest of the world? For better or worse, how would it be possible to keep closed a country of such size and potential? Mao's bold attempt to "create" the new man belonged to a utopia, but the attempt had had to be made. Now, at the beginning of the 1980s, after an enormous social and political upheaval, the time was right for a real leap forward, the greatest leap imaginable. The conditions were right, the privations and the spirit of collective solidarity, for better or worse, had produced results. Deng Xiaoping returned to the scene, the man of reform, the advocate of another audacious attempt, that of creating a socialist market economy with a strong dose of Confucianism. Beijing emerged from the experiment of the "new" man to find itself leading the experiment of the "four modernisations". I was a witness to this epoch-making shift, which appealed to the necessity to open both minds and frontiers. It was no longer a question of "better Red than expert", but rather "it doesn't matter if the cat is white or grey, as long as it catches mice". Judgement was passed over recent history by the reviled "Gang of Four". Court decisions established that Chairman Mao was the architect of the new China, and that his actions had been "seventy percent good, and thirty percent wrong". After the excesses, and even madness, of the Cultural Revolution it was recognised that it was necessary to re-enter the world. Deng's China embarked on the great miracle of modernisation. With the slogan "to make China a rich and modern country by the year 2000", the second great revolution, which was to complete the epic cycle of a century, got under way. "There is no doubt that the next century will be China's century", Mao had prophesied in the 1950s. His prophesy was right.

In the summer of 1986, I decided to celebrate the tenth anniversary of my first trip with an adventure involving my whole family. In a journey that was memorable for all four of us, we took the Trans-Siberian Express from Moscow and, having crossed the entire Eurasian continent, arrived in Beijing a week later. My daughters were fourteen and eleven, an ideal age for a journey of this kind, even if my wife had many quite reasonable reservations. Our arrival in Beijing on a humid morning in July was like reaching an objective that had seemed unattainable. For someone who has never experienced it, it is impossible to imagine what seven days and seven nights on a train is like, nine thousand kilometres of railways. Living in the train the whole time, eating, sleeping, waiting, watching. The interminable landscape we crossed was still the Soviet Union with all its restrictions and obsessive police controls. Our contact with the irrational rules and regulations of Russian communism was an education for us. Before we had even left Jaroslavskaja Station in Moscow, we had had our first run in with "ideological" stupidity. The taxi driver, booked by Inturist, the Russian tourist agency, was taking us to the wrong station, Minskaja, which meant we would miss the train, which left only once a week, our visas would expire, and we would have to give up the journey. When I realised we were going the wrong way, I pulled the keys from the ignition and yelled "Jaroslavskaja! Jaroslavskaja!"; thanks heavens I had found out from which of the many Moscow stations the Trans-Siberian left. Having deposited the family and our bags on the pavement, I now had to choose between two stations, one opposite the other. The problem was soon solved by presenting a handful of roubles to a porter who, understanding our situation, had rushed forward with his cart to offer his services. "Sibiria, Kitai, Pekin", I said, and with another tip for the policeman who was controlling the gate, our little caravan entered the station and ran to the platform. The immensely long train for "Pekin", in the mythical Catai, as the Russians still call China, stood waiting. When we found the right carriage, two icy female ticket collectors, who barred the way and checked our tickets, rudely informed us that we would have to separate: wife and daughters in one carriage, myself in another. How could they be so stupid when our booking was quite clearly for two compartments next to each other with a communicating door? A mistake had been made, but it couldn't be corrected as no one had the necessary authority. The train was about to leave, and there was no time to be lost. I threw myself into the compartments we had booked, and called for the train's controller, who after a long argument agreed that we could stay together. As we crossed Russia and Siberia, we continued to distribute roubles, and our situation began to improve. We ate magnificently in the restaurant car. A Chinese theatre company, however, returning from an Eastern European tour, were repeatedly and brutally refused entry. I don't know how they survived for a week. In the stations where we stopped there was nothing to buy except a few tins of fish, and the local residents came to the train to buy bread from the restaurant car, which turned into a kind of shop.

When we arrived in China everything changed: at Manzhoulì station, we were welcomed by a band, and the shops were overflowing with goods. Beijing greeted us with its endless chaotic outskirts, and around the Dongbianmen tower, which stood like a sailing ship run aground amidst the reefs of the little houses under demolition, the building sites were teeming with activity in what was to become the financial district of Jianguomen. The initial impact on my family was astounding: the difference between Beijing and our little provincial town near Venice was total. What had become familiar to me, for my daughters was absolutely new, was different and was fun. They soon picked up a few words in Chinese, learned to eat with chopsticks, and noted in their diaries all the strange things they saw. For them it was the beginning of the ongoing process of "understanding" China.

It was in that summer that I became friends with Lu Xin, the man who over the years has been quite indispensable to my entering into the complex reality of China. I had a friend who was the head of an important group of high quality restaurants, and I had brought with me his idea of opening the first Italian restaurant in Beijing. Lu Xin worked for the Chinese partner, the State Tourist Agency, and was one of the young managers of the Beijing International Hotel under construction at the time. We met at a banquet that was held in my honour. I was immediately taken by his open cordiality and clear desire to communicate. He was just over thirty, married to the daughter of a diplomat, and had a three-year-old daughter whom we came to know as Lucia. A former Red Guard, fully reformed but in some way nostalgic , the only son of an English teacher and a secretary, a graduate in Spanish, fascinated by electronic technology (cameras, video-cameras, and later mobile phones, computers, sat navs). When he explained to me that his name, Xin, meant "industrious", I realised that I had stumbled upon a very special person. Xiao Lu, as I called him because he was younger than me, was the right person, in the right place, at the right time: I could not have imagined anyone better. His intuitions were acute, he was always quick to find solutions, able to mediate between conflicting attitudes, always up-to-the-minute about what was going on, flexible in his judgments, never dogmatic, possessed of the greatest common sense, and always ready to give way if a situation seemed fruitless. Lu Xin was, and is, my Virgil in my complex journey through the past, present and future of Beijing. I honestly don't know how much I could have understood without him, the precious companion of my visits and travels in his country. We have been everywhere together, from the remote provinces of Xinjiang to Heilongjiang, from Mongolia to Tibet, from Gansu to the island of Hainan. But it is above all in Beijing, the Beijing always so full of surprises, that his friendship has been so constantly invaluable.

Xiao Lu and Lao Ma (this is the Chinese name that he gave me), for our many friends and acquaintances, are quite inseparable. Over the years we have created our own language that no one else can understand: a mixture of Chinese, English, Spanish, and Veneto dialect. We use the first word which comes into our heads. This strange combination of languages leads to fast communication, and we use it all the time, especially at dinner when the confusion becomes magnificence. If we use English words, the pronunciation is entirely our own, either Italianised or as if the words were Chinese, and the result is incomprehensible to anyone else. We feel that a language is merely a key that opens the way for communication. And so we are concerned with neither grammatical nor pronunciation errors. We simply want to open the door and understand each other.

In our strange language, we can communicate the most delicate shades of meaning, or our slightest intuitions or a sense of complicity, so that with just one word we understand each other perfectly, or one word can capture an opinion about the person before us or the circumstances of the moment. Lu Xin was my irreplaceable "property man" during my journey through the transformation of Beijing. This role is normally that of the indispensable assistant to a film director: you need a uniform from the War of Independence? a 17th-century Spanish armchair? a car from 1910? a field telephone? a gramophone, a gladiator's helmet, a 13th-century parchment? He's the guy you ask. Your "property man". Well, Lu Xin was, and still is today, the man who, quite incredibly, found everything that I asked for, not just things, but people too. And what people! In the chaos of a capital transformed into a building site, with whole areas that from one day to the next fell to the bulldozers and the dynamite, with hutung that were swallowed up by the rubble, and the names of streets and districts which disappeared for ever from the maps of the city, Lu Xin managed to find, amongst many others, a craftsman who had made a wooden model of Imperial Beijing, a painter whose whereabouts no one knew who had last been heard of during the Cultural Revolution, and no less a personage than the widow of the last emperor, Pu Yi, living alone in anonymity in a block of flats scheduled for demolition.

In those years, I became fascinated by research into the monuments and buildings of Old Beijing, and particularly by a survey I wanted to make of what had been left intact after the planning initiatives of the 1950s and 60s, when the city walls and fourteen of the sixteen old city gates had disappeared. The Dongbianmen Tower, miraculously still intact, suggested that I could start looking for traces of the old walls behind the low houses and run-down blocks of flats that had been built along an east-west axis as far as Chongwenmen, in front of my first hotel, the Xin Qiao. I didn't want to involve Lu Xin in my researches, as I knew it might be inopportune for him to be seen to be accompanying a "waiguoren" to those rather sordid areas, or to get involved in any controversy regarding the obtuse and irresponsible planning decisions. So I went alone, in the early morning,

armed with my camera and determined to get through that sad barrier of hovels and barrack-like buildings, passing through courtyards and alleyways under the understandably suspicious gaze of the local inhabitants. I was amazed, however, to find that the walls were still there, that the ugly buildings had simply been placed on top of them, or rather that the very bricks of the old walls had been used to build the new houses. This aberration was not limited to the area around the Dongbianmen Tower, but continued for at least two kilometres as far as Chongwenmen. By ruthlessly tearing down everything that had been built next to the Tartar walls and their bastions, by knocking down all those houses and blocks of flats, by recovering all the bricks that had been used to create that muddle of construction, it would be possible to give back to Beijing those massive defensive walls which had for centuries been one of its great marvels. I took part in a debate which sparked off furious argument in the papers and in the Beijing City Council, and some time later, what had seemed quite impossible actually began to happen: houses and blocks of flats were knocked down, more than two million old bricks were recovered, ancient acacia trees were saved, and the "Park of the Ming Walls" was created which, for many years now, has been a place for walks and quiet reflection for the elderly.

With the enthusiasm of the neophyte, from that moment, my friend was fired by an enthusiasm for all things "ancient", and he followed me in my search for the old city which, strangely, from day to day, re-emerged from where it had been swallowed up by the inadequate and disorganised building of the revolutionary years. It was then that I decided to organise my research into the re-emerging past by making a detailed study of the old maps for a publishing project entitled "Beijing, the capital of the Heavenly Empire", a project which I am still working on today. The editor of the magazine Beijing This Month allowed me some space for an article regarding my historical research and my "discoveries". My Beijing experience was enriched by passing the Chinese New Year on a number of occasions with Lu Xin and his family in the old temples which have been restored and reopened: a wonderful way to enter into the immutable heart of the city, its places, its entertainments and its food. As the new city grew, so did the nostalgia for its past, the desire to recapture the spirit of the ancient capital of marvels. But mark those words, to recapture the spirit, not its physical aspect.

Beijing was undergoing rapid change, and during the hundred journeys I made in the 1980s and 90s, I witnessed the dragon change its skin. Day by day, Beijing almost lost the romantic and relaxed feel of the leafy outskirts, and turned into a great metropolis of the twenty-first century. Each time I went, whole areas had disappeared, including the beautiful siheyuan, and this in itself opened wounds which were destined to cause their own pain one day. Because it was clear that after the destruction someone, one day,

would become aware of the loss, and those old houses would be rebuilt. This has happened all over Beijing in the last few years, not only around the Forbidden City and the Drum Tower, but also on a large scale in Qianmen, where a whole district, including the tram, has been recreated the way it was in the early 20th century. A replica of Yongdingmen, the southern gate of the outer city and the entrance to Beijing from the south, demolished during the seventies, was built on precisely the same spot in the early years of the 21st century. There is already talk of rebuilding Dianmen, while the internal walls, with their reddish-purple plaster and yellow roof tiles, have re-emerged following the demolition of the houses that had been built alongside them. The nostalgia of the people of Beijing for their magnificent old capital is very strong as parts of it reappear, and some of its most emblematic buildings are rebuilt. But at the time of the first "modernisation", not only were the old Tartar houses of the hutung swept away down, but so were the ancient acacias whose trunks, as sacred as any buildings, preserved the memory of the Empire. The romance disappeared, but so did a great deal of the poverty, and it was inevitable that an urban project for a more civilised and modern existence would have its victims. In Beijing there was a shortage of good housing, with running water and toilets, a shortage of roads and sewers, and the electricity network, a spider's web of wires above the head, was primitive; everything had to be organised, to be rebuilt, to be made to work.

Thirty years of autocratic government had guaranteed the survival and, in fact, the doubling of the population, but this in itself had become a problem. With the slogan, "well fed and well dressed", Mao had achieved his first aim of feeding and clothing everyone, even if only with a bowl of rice and a cotton tunic: what mattered was not to die of starvation as in the past. In 1949 the disaster was total, everywhere there was utter poverty and famine, and death rates were sky high. Now population growth had to be slowed down by controlling the birth rate; this was the wise policy of the reformers of the 1980s. Beijing, too, had to follow the rules in order to achieve an increase in living standards, to reduce the pressure of an abnormal population and to plan the new city. The reforms would allow the construction of houses, roads, hospitals, schools and refectories; they would lead to the improvement of public transport and services, and the creation of jobs for all even if only humble jobs paying little more than a few yuan. As a witness to this truly revolutionary fervour, on journey after journey, I observed the transformation of Beijing's appearance into that of a modern capital with its luxury hotels ready for the tourist invasion. The breakneck rush into the 21st century had caused the destruction of a great part of the "local colour" that, in reality, was mostly represented by inhospitable hovels where the elderly, quite understandably, clung to the past. My soul, that had loved the hutung and the ancient acacias, was in turmoil, but my rational mind realised that poverty was a state that had to be given up, that there was a limit to tolerance, and that it must be overcome at any price, even at the risk of inevitable speculation. Beijing was overwhelmed, and skyscrapers and cranes sprouted up all round the horizon. It was gradually becoming unrecognisable, an endless building sight where I observed the future taking shape in its myriad forms. China was overrun by a wave of modernity stronger than a hundred earthquakes. The decrepit old city fell apart under the power of the wrecking ball. I walked through the rubble where teams of workers piled up the ancient blackened beams and ash-grey bricks in scenes reminiscent of a city after a bombardment. Where the hutung had been swept away, amongst the torment of real feeling and of sentimentalism, there arose roads, bridges, tower blocks, and squares with all the dignity of a smart city. The people themselves changed too. Not only in their clothes, which had now reached European standards, but in their habits and behaviour. I don't honestly know if they are any happier, that is a matter for the sociologists, but today I no longer meet the affectionate, anonymous people that I met thirty years ago. They will, however, always be in my heart, and in the photographs that I took at the time, and for their permission to take them, whether they reacted in amazement, or posed happily as the old people and the children usually did, I shall always be grateful.

In October 1988, I returned to Beijing after a seven-day trip to North Korea. The days were beautifully sunny and the leaves had turned to yellow. Lu Xin invited me to take a relaxing stroll behind the Bell Tower, in a quiet area of hutung that still survived. We walked for over a hour and suddenly found ourselves in a street bounded on one side by a thick, high wall overhung by the highest branches of ancient acacias, and on the other by lower walls enclosing old siheyuan. The street was narrow, and we couldn't see what lay beyond the wall. But suddenly I could "see", as if the wall were transparent, everything that was on the other side. I asked Lu Xin if he knew what there was beyond the wall, but he didn't know. I felt paralysed by the sensation that I knew exactly what was there, and I "saw" a large garden with enormous stones, mounds covered in trees and bushes, and a series of wooden pavilions with pointed grey roofs and parapets carved with bat motifs. In the centre of a small lake, stood an open-sided structure with a canopy joined to the bank by a small wooden bridge. I described everything to the astonished Lu Xi, and I told him that though I had never been to this garden, everything seemed extraordinarily familiar. Amazed by my description, he said that we absolutely had to go and see. The only entrance was a huge and solid iron door secured with locks and chains. Not far away was a bicycle repair shop, and Lu Xin told me to wait while he went to get some information. I stood staring at that wall, which seemed to draw me into its mystery, and through which I had "seen", as if I already knew perfectly what lay behind it. Nothing like this had happened to me before, and I felt a strange sense of disquiet. After a few minutes, Lu Xin came back accompanied by an old man gesticulating broadly, and when they reached me he asked me to repeat my vision. One by one I told him the things I had seen, and while Lu Xin translated, the old man made little cries of amazement as his bright eyes flashed. He looked me up and down, and began to open the door. He was the guardian. When we entered, I felt once again that I had already been there. But when? Never. Everything was exactly as I had "seen" and described, even down to the smallest details of the bats carved on the balustrade. The further we went into that abandoned place, with tiles that had slid from the roofs and smashed on the stone walkways, the more I was filled with a sense of euphoria and well-being, incredulous at what had happened. The old man told me that it had been the house of Prince Kung, who died in 1898, the brother of the unfortunate Emperor Xienfeng. I knew virtually nothing about him, and at the time no map of Beijing showed that ancient residence (as indeed they didn't show many major buildings that hadn't been restored). As we left, Lu Xin kept repeating that the whole thing was just incredible. I won't continue with this tale now except to add that over the years that followed I developed a strange and mysterious relationship with the story. After thirteen years of fruitless research, I finally managed to track down, in a somewhat unusual way, the diplomatic document-case of the Marquis, Giuseppe Salvago Raggi, Italian ambassador to Beijing at the time of the Boxer Rebellion. I had been looking for the documents in order to reconstruct the history of that event, and when the famous case finally came into my possession, I was reminded of the mysterious episode that had taken place in Beijing thirteen years earlier. My experience then became connected with the discovery of the case on the Monferrato hills. Amongst the many important documents found in the case was the diary of the ambassador, in which I read that Prince Kung had been to see him at the Italian Legation, and that he had promised to repay the visit. A few months later, however, the Prince had died. Quite unconsciously, these two episodes - my "vision" and the discovery of the document case - became linked in my mind, and associated with a mysterious scent of flowers in a way that was almost surreal. I realised that there was something special in all this when I discovered that the scent, that I detected at quite random moments, even when I was at home in Italy, was the scent of the acacias of Beijing, those of the garden of Prince Kung, an island of the past besieged by the modernising city.

Before the end of the century, after the return of Hong Kong to China in 1997, I stepped up my research into ancient Beijing, partly because I perceived the serious danger of the loss of the city's old identity; the city that had been described by western travellers of the early 20th century as "absurd", the quintessence of the topsy-turvy Chinese world that it was impossible to understand. I realised that, on the contrary, the old Beijing had been a kind of "ideal city", built in homage to a complex geomancy inspired by Taoism following a geometric theorem originating in some form of divination. For me Beijing was the child of some arcane system, and I had to decipher it in order to understand it. I was interested in understanding how it had reached breaking point with the West, and why there was so much incomprehension and mutual suspicion. The Boxer Rebellion of the summer of 1900 had been preceded by great hostility towards China, and followed by ferocious repression involving Beijing in the humiliation of roadside executions, looting and the dismantling of its magnificent architecture. I had become convinced that this was at the base of its tragic break with the West. I wasn't convinced by the representation of those tragic events that I had read in the books of certain historians (and certain pseudo-historians), which ended invariably with the arrival of the good guys, i.e. "Us", just like the cavalry saving everyone from the Indians in a western. When I read in a book by the Englishman, Peter Fleming, that the Italian ambassador Salvago Raggi "was the only man in the Legations who continued to dress for dinner", and that this was the only reference generously reserved to our diplomatic representative, I began to look for documents that I knew must be preserved in some dusty archive or forgotten attic. That note, sounding like a line from a popular song, about the "man who continued to dress for dinner" had instilled in me the suspicion that he must have been not only a stickler for form, but also a real gentleman, so that getting my hands on his papers, and the flimsy pages of his dispatches, or perhaps even his memoirs would probably allow me to rewrite a fundamental episode in the history of Beijing. In that document case, I found the proof that things had gone a little differently, and that the mysterious link with Prince Kung was more a matter of destiny than of plain circumstances. The famous afternoon of my "vision" had remained etched on my memory, framed in the golden glow of the autumn leaves. There came a night when the wind swept down from Mongolia, and screamed at my bedroom window like a furious demon. It sounded like the lamentation of the damned, of a chorus of infinitely unhappy ghosts. I couldn't sleep, and lay listening as the idea of the ghosts ran through my mind; I heard their mournful cries which fused together in an infinite spiral of pain. I had often thought of Beijing as a spirit world, where on windy nights the ghosts of generations lament how their world had been so utterly transformed. Perhaps Prince Kung was amongst them. By the following morning winter had arrived. The bare trees stood out starkly against the sky, and the street cleaners had swept the leaves up into great yellow piles. This is what happens in Beijing: the winter arrives after a windy night which strips the acacias bare, leaving as a

mere memory the autumn of the day before.

At the beginning of the new century, the transformation of the city took on an American flavour. The proliferation of McDonald's and Kentucky Fried Chicken attracted the young people like magnets. Along with Western fast food (officially frowned upon), I was also amazed to see how milk, completely alien to the traditional Chinese diet, suddenly became popular too. It had always been said that the Chinese race didn't have the necessary enzymes to digest lactose, but with the arrival of the new century, the tastes and diets of the new generations were rapidly modified. First in the diplomatic district of San Li Tun, then along the Huo Hai lake, and finally more or less everywhere, but especially in the up-and-coming district of Chaoyang, bars and night clubs sprung up with jazz and rock music playing until dawn, and alcohol flowing in rivers. Big, foreign cars and sophisticated toilets were all part of the new public display of wealth; the hedonism of the East has always been more garish and more blatant than that in the West.

The provinces, where progress is slow, still lived deep in the past, and many young people arrived in Beijing attracted by the allure of TV advertising, which showed a capital of bright lights and new opportunities. Migration from sleepy, traditional cities far away, the initial impact with the city which never lived up to expectations, and the distrust of the people of Beijing towards the adventurers of liberalisation all created a palpable social tension, a resentment of those who sought not only their fortune, but also the thrills of the big city, and contributed to the debasement of the ancient character of Beijing. The atmosphere changed rapidly. On one hand, there were the people of Beijing with their affection for the city that was disappearing in the face of modernisation, with their affection for the hard "R" of their cultivated dialect, lovers of the theatre and the opera, and the fading glories of the past which only in Beijing had a true "Imperial" flavour. On the other, there were the new arrivals, full of atavistic aversion for the ancient parasitic capital, but determined to find their fortune there, improvising any kind of job merely to survive. The foreigners, arriving from the four corners of the earth like wasps attracted to honey, organised a parallel life for themselves, and lived in their own private bubble, protected by their passports and their deep pockets. Only the occasional "mad" expert on China had ever tried to fit into the life of the capital, making a show of adopting just the right customs and habits, but they were rarely more than off-the-wall mavericks. The others, all the others, had rapidly reconstructed their own little worlds convinced of their superiority. Beijing and China, in the meantime, were going through a metamorphosis, and when the chrysalis opened, its unstoppable power provoked consternation and fear.

The West has still to realise quite how much China has changed, despite the fact that it can still only be compared to itself. It seems paradoxical that my experience of over thirty years has led me to this conclusion: that there is an unbridgeable abyss between my first journey in the spring of 1976 and my most recent one in the autumn of 2008. The changes are in some way radical, and yet the "spirit" of China has remained enigmatic, more linked to its remote past than its more recent past. It is wrong to think that Beijing has become like any modern "western" city; on the contrary, it is the most important "Asiatic" city, the epitome of what Asia wishes to be, and is quite right in wishing to be, a model for a new and different civilisation. The Chinese model bears similarity only to itself, and this is the great virtue that we in the West have to understand. With unimaginable speed, China is reclaiming the place it had in the world until 1839, and that was taken from it by aggressive, colonial wars. Its place as the supreme world power. In the mid-19th century, it had been, for thousands of years, the greatest economic and cultural power in the world. Today it is also becoming the greatest political and military power.

When Mao the ideologue, in prophetic vein, declared that "the wind from the East will overcome the wind from the West", he was undoubtedly thinking of the primacy of revolution (China) over reaction (the West); but since Mao, as the expert Taoist philosopher that he clearly was, was able to say one thing and its precise opposite at the same time, he could also easily have imagined the future primacy of China over the rest of the world all of which, for him, was the West. These thoughts come to me spontaneously precisely because I have lived through the thirty years which have seen "the sky put into the earth, and the earth put into the sky", to once again paraphrase Mao, the man who, for better or for worse, was the engine for the profoundest change, through the reaction that he sparked off amongst his people who, since time immemorial, had been steeped in the darkest resignation and the pernicious philosophy of non action. Now China is on the march, bursting with unstoppable vitality. And there is no reason why it should stop. The interesting problem is to understand to what extent this process has influenced, and still influences, not only the existential models of the Chinese, but also their ancient culture, the DNA of a people who, for more than seventy generations, have absorbed a vision of life which has developed separately to our own. Beijing is the touchstone for our interpretation of a world we find hard to grasp, which easily confuses us. But our interpretation may yet be wrong; our readings have become more simplistic, and are simplified according to our own models of existence. This is the age-old problem of being happy to judge by appearances, by the superficial things.

But if we look carefully at the great city of Beijing, it is clear that much of its life has really not changed so much. The backdrop has changed, the scenery is now that of the enormous, futuristic skyscrapers, sacred to the canons of modern architecture, but the real spirit of the people of Beijing is the same. You can still buy goldfish in the courtyards of Ritan, the Temple of the Sun, where the old people bring their singing golden orioles in bamboo cages. My trained eye does not miss all those little details of the old Beijing that have not been lost, of the Lao Beijing romanticised in the chic salons of the new bourgeoisie. In the old Imperial parks, in the shade of the thuja trees, the old traditions are still followed. On feast days, if you enter the Temple of Heaven by the east gate, the singers and players of the Opera are still here in the open air surrounded by their fans, while row upon row of choristers practice to the rhythm of the nostalgic revolutionary marches. And Ditan, the Temple of the Earth, is still the place for the competitions between the crickets imprisoned in their little carved gourds, while the skilled spinners of tops fill the air with mournful but harmonious whistling. And in Tian'anmen, the ingenious kites still fly: rapacious birds, fish with great, winged tails, and long dragons rising into the sky in competition on any windy day in Beijing. 1978 or 2008? What does it matter? In Beijing it is still the same.

With the 2008 Olympic Games, I was again witness to the extraordinary scale of the change that has taken place in Beijing and China. Arriving at the capital's new airport was, once again, like arriving on a different planet, and comparing this moment to my arrival in 1976 was enough to make my head spin. The leap forward that Beijing and China have made is quite astounding, and in the years of my first journeys, even imagining progress of this nature was utterly inconceivable. I observe the disbelieving faces of the foreigners arriving for the first time in China as they enter the new Beijing airport: however much they might have heard about the modernisation of this enormous country, the impact of the new reality is overwhelming. After 155 separate journeys to this country, I can truthfully say that I have witnessed every stage in its recent changes. But even I, arriving in the new airport, cannot but feel enraptured by the image of the modernity which has now overtaken the whole of China. No airport in the world can bear comparison with this one, and it is unlikely that any other city in the world can offer an array of structures and facilities as modern and efficient as those in Beijing: motorways, viaducts, skyscrapers, hotels, shopping centres and residential areas. In today's world Beijing is synonymous with modernity, and this splendid capital has become the quintessence of the achievable, offering glimpses of the world to come.

The 2008 Olympiad was an opportunity for China to demonstrate that it is serious in its intent: the Games went ahead smoothly in an atmosphere of security and efficiency. The fact that everything worked to perfection was proof of the maturity of Beijing, and of its primacy of place amongst international cities. To see all this, and to compare it with what I saw more than thirty years ago fills me with joy in my friendship with the Chinese people, and intensifies my relationship with this great city, with "my" Beijing, which has remained one of the most fascinating destinations on the planet: in 1976, because it was closed, mysterious and unknown; in 2008, because it is open, a visible laboratory for those who have eyes to see, itself a witness to the modern times which will come to us all, both here and beyond the Great Wall, a symbol, no longer of division, but of the union between China and the rest of the world.

改革前夜（1976 — 1977）
Before Reform

老首都机场。摄于1976年4月30日到北京后的一个早晨。红底白字的标语牌写的是：庆祝五一国际劳动节。前厅放置了一座毛泽东的石膏塑像，一些国内航班的旅客们在此排队等候登机。The old airport of the capital on the morning of my arrival in Beijing, 30 April 1976. The white ideograms on a red background celebrate Mayday, the international holiday. In the entrance hall, dominated by a plaster-cast statue of Mao, a group of passengers wait for an internal flight. 📷

五一节下午，人头攒动的天安门广场。天安门是中华人民共和国的象征，1949 年 10 月 1 日毛泽东在城楼上宣告了中华人民共和国成立。两边的红色标语牌为："中华人民共和国万岁" 和 " 世界人民大团结万岁"。

Crowded Mayday afternoon in Tian'anmen Square, with the Gate of Heavenly Peace, the symbol of the People's Republic of China founded by Mao Zedong on 1 October 1949 and proclaimed from the balcony above his image. The ideograms on the two large red panels read: "Ten thousand years to the People's Republic of China", and "Ten thousand years to the union of the peoples of the world". 📷

天安门广场东侧，一座大型的中国国家博物馆
（中国历史博物馆）。

下图：那时小孩很流行穿"开裆"裤，现在在城
市几乎已经看不到了。裤子下裆是完全开敞着
的，要穿到3岁左右。"尿不湿"是以后才出现的。

Tian'anmen Square with, on its eastern side, the
enormous Museum of Chinese History and
Civilisation.

Underside:The once typical, but now disappearing
in city, "open" underpants and shorts of children up
to the age of three, with bottoms on full display.
Nappies are thing of the future. 📷

长安街天安门广场东侧地段,到处是人群和自行车,在那个时期,除了公共汽车外,很难见到小轿车。

Crowds of pedestrians and cyclists in Chang'an Avenue (Everlasting Peace) at the eastern entrance to Tian'anmen Square, the route of buses and the very occasional car. 📷

人民大会堂，也就是国家议会，位于天安门广场的西侧。正面悬挂着毛泽东的画像，它是人民共和国的象征。在画像的两侧，悬挂的红色标语牌上写着："领导我们事业的核心力量是中国共产党，指导我们思想的理论基础是马克思列宁主义"。

下图: 人民英雄纪念碑前广场上的人群和人民大会堂。

The Palace of the People's Assembly, the seat of Parliament, lies on the western side of Tian'anmen Square. The facade carries the portrait of Mao alongside the emblem of the People's Republic. The red vertical panel reads: "The guiding body of our cause is the Chinese Communist Party. The theoretical base which guides our thoughts is Marxist-Leninism".

Underside: Crowds in Tian'anmen Square in front of the Monument to the Heroes of the People and the Palace of the People's Assembly. 📷

在天安门广场，上生动的历史课，学生们在讲解
人民英雄纪念碑台基上的表现中国革命运动的浮
雕群像。

下图：在观礼台销售《人民日报号外》，观礼台
曾是军政界代表们观看群众游行的地方。

Tian'anmen Square. Outdoor lesson explaining the
reliefs representing the Chinese revolution at the
base of the Monument to the Heroes of the People.

Underside: Sale of a special edition of Renmin Ribao
(the People's Daily) from the space reserved for
those invited to political and military parades. 📷

天安门广场上，老人推着用轴承作轱辘的自造小推车在散步，车上坐着小孙女儿。

下图：正阳门，位于天安门广场的南侧，门楼上悬挂的标语上写着："继承毛主席的遗志，把无产阶级革命事业进行到底！"正阳门俗称"前门"，在明清帝王时期，是皇城的正南门。

Tian'anmen Square. Taking the grandchildren out for some air in a pushchair with domestically produced ball bearings.

Underside: Zhengyangmen Gate, on the south side of Tian'anmen Square, with the words: "We must follow the thoughts of President Mao and continue the class struggle until the end". Zhengyangmen, also Rnown as Qianmen Gate, was the main entrance to the "Imperial City" in imperial times. 📷

从"汉人城"（指北京城的外城）看到的前门。城楼上一条鼓舞人民的标语："高举毛泽东思想伟大红旗奋勇前进！"前门大街就是从这里开始一直延伸到天坛，它曾是古都的商业街。

下图：前门东大街上行走的红卫兵和骑自行车者。

The Qianmen Gate seen from the "Chinese City". The people are incited by the words: "We must hold high the great red flag of Mao Zedong's thought and go forward". From this gate Qianmen Avenue leads to the Temple of Heaven crossing what was once the commercial area of the ancient capital.

Underside: Pedestrians with Red Guards and cyclists in Qianmen Dong Avenue. 📷

北京火车站的早晨。

下图：远处，旅客正等待售票处开门。

Early morning at the railway station.

Underside: Travellers waiting for the ticket office to open.

西单北大街早上的自行车流,道路两旁种满了槐树，这是北京街道的特有景观。

Morning bicycle traffic in Xidan Bei Avenue shaded by typical acacias of Beijing streets. 📷

拥挤的东单北大街,这是一条和西边王府井大街平行的商业街, 在大照片中, 人们的背后, 就是东单和东长安街的汇合处。

Everyday bustle in Dongdan Bei Avenue, the commercial street to the west and parallel to the central Wangfujing Street. In the large photo, at their backs, is the confluence with the eastern section of Chang'an Avenue. 📷

北京城南的一条街道，两旁的房屋已经很破旧。
下图：一骑自行车者，好奇地停下来望着我。这
是在长安街北京饭店附近，当时北京饭店是首都
最高的建筑。

A street in the southern outskirts with dilapidated
houses.

Underside: A cyclist, curioused about my presence,
in Chang'an Avenue, near the Beijing Hotel, the
highest building in the capital at the time. 📷

西单一个自行车商店前,售货员们都盯着那个戴着白手套显得很自豪的摩托车车主看。

下图: 某街道办事处的大门口,一幅巨大的横匾上有"为人民服务"这几个大字,这是毛泽东题词手迹。

In front of a bicycle shop in Xidan, the attention of shop assistants is caught by a real rarity: a motorcycle proudly ridden by its owner in white gloves.

Underside: The entrance to a district office of the Communist Party with the famous words, "To serve the people", reproduced in Mao's handwriting. 📷

一个系着红领巾的女学生从学校走出来。

下图：一个靠近农贸市场和商业区的路边自行车停放处。

在西单北大街人行道上，学生们在等公交车。

Schoolgirl with the red handkerchief of the "pioneers" returning from school.

Underside: One of the innumerable bicycle parks alongside the roads near markets and commercial areas.

On the pavement of Xidan Bei Avenue, waiting for bus. 📷

邻近长安街的建国门地区一条胡同的清晨生活景象。

Scenes of early morning life in the hutung of the Jianguomen area near Chang'an Avenue. 📷

胡同普通生活一景。一直到90年代兴建高楼大
厦之前，这里俨然是都市里的村庄。

Here and following pages: scenes of everyday life
in the hutung, the warren of alleyways which, until
they were overwhelmed by the building boom of
the Nineties, made up the urban fabric of the city,
making it appear like an immense country village.

远离喧闹和拥挤的胡同里的生活是简单愉快的，
非常近似乡村生活。

Far from the noise and the traffic, life in the hutung
was simple and quiet, and went on much as it did in
the countryside. 📷

一位工人正忙着给各家各户送蜂窝煤,用于取暖及做饭。

下图: 平板车上的篮子里盛满了新鲜的切面 (传统的面条),准备销售给附近的居民。

A worker delivered coal for heating and cooking,
Underside: Abarrow laden with baskets of fresh
noodles (the traditional "miantiao") ready for home
delivery.

人们在排队买新鲜面条,这在当时不是每天都会
供应的。
下图: 位于旧使馆区附近台基厂的商店刚刚到了
一车冻猪肉。

Queue to buy fresh noodles, a product not available
everyday.

Underside: The arrival of frozen pork at a shop in
Taijichang Avenue in the former Legation District.

在故宫城墙下，一位老人独自在晨练。
一位女教师带领一群人有节奏地在练习太极拳，
太极拳起源于古老的哲学。

 Morning gymnastics performed alone, along the im-
posing walls of the Forbidden City, or in a group
with an instructress beating the time. Tai chi: the
ritual gymnastics inspired by ancient philosophy.

📷

一个小"红卫兵"在故宫留影。故宫,意为旧日的宫殿,就是著名的紫禁城。

A very young Red Guard in the courtyards of Gu Gong, the Old Palace, as the Forbidden City is known. 📷

他们是普通老百姓，有很多是农民，从很远的地方来到故宫参观。他们对能够来到帝王时代任何普通人都不能进入的圣地上游览感到很知足。

下图：一个用白色毛巾做成的很有特点的帽子，说明这个游客是来自中国北方的农民。

Common people, including many peasants who have come from the most distant regions to visit the Forbidden City, stroll with satisfaction through the sacred places once forbidden to any mortal being.

Underside: The typical head-covering made from a white towel shows that this visitor is a peasant from the north of china. 📷

台基厂大街上北京市委大楼对面的邮递员。背景是北京饭店。邮递员的邮包里装满了报纸：那时没有报刊亭，且只有三种主要报纸（《人民日报》、《光明日报》和《工人日报》），而且只能到邮局订阅，由邮递员来派送。

The arrival of the postman in front of the headquarters of the Communist Party in Taijichang Street. The Beijing Hotel dominates the scene. The postman's bags are full of newspapers: newsstands do not exist and the three newspapers that are available (Renmin Ribao, Guangming Ribao and the Workers' Daily) can only be bought by postal subscription or home delivery. 📷

一巨幅油画展现了毛主席与他的接班人华国锋的谈话情景。

下图：天坛集会。

Looking almost like a votive chapel, a stand with the great picture of Mao in conversation with his successor Hua Guofeng.

Underside: In Temple of Heaven 📷

在天坛一座官殿屋檐下，一群女"红卫兵"在观看学生们为庆祝五一准备的歌舞表演。

In the shadow of the great curved roof of one of the pavilions of the Temple of Heaven, a packed group of female "Red Guards" watches the theatrical performances and ballets prepared by groups of schoolchildren for the beginning of Mayday. 📷

一群学生在天坛表演革命节目，这是在首都所有公园庆祝五一劳动节的活动之一。

A school band performs revolutionary anthems at the Temple of Heaven as part of the Mayday celebrations which take place in all the parks of the capital.

崭露新机（1978—1988）
Change

很多人在观看"大字报"，当时所谓的"民主墙"是位于西单的一个汽车总站前面的一堵墙，上面贴满了大字报。在 1979 年春天，在邓小平复出掌权后，进行了许多改革，却遭到了不公正的谩骂和指责。

Crowd reading the "dazibao": protests pasted to the so-called "Wall of Democracy", in front of a bus park on Fuxingmen Wei. In the spring of 1979, en-couraged by the return to power of Deng Xiaoping, many took advantage of the promise of reform, by denouncing abuses and injustice. 📷

骑着自行车的人们在一个路口停下。可以看出邓小平权力恢复后已经出现一些细小的变化：彩色的外套，流行款式的墨镜，一件防水衣，一件浅色外套。用彩色的丝巾蒙脸，当然，这是老习惯，是为了避免春天从蒙古高原吹来的风沙的袭击。Cyclists at a stop sign waiting to set off. A few minor changes brought about by Deng's coming to power can already be observed: a coloured jacket, a pair of fashionable modern sunglasses, a raincoat and a non-regulation light jacket. The coloured headscarves are, however, part of an ancient tradition and protect their wearers from the sands of the Mongolian plateau brought down by the spring winds. 📷

(20世纪) 70年代末，露天菜市场迅速蔓延到整个城市，甚至到了市中心。这里是前门外一个老字号丝绸店对面的菜场。

下图：菜市场和从农村来的街头商贩："文化大革命"后允许农民成为"自由职业者"，市民们很高兴能够买到比国营市场物美价廉的蔬菜。

In the late Seventies, the free vegetable markets spread rapidly throughout the city, even into the centre: here we are just outside Qianmen Gate, in front of the famous silk shop.

Underside: Vegetable market and street sellers from the countryside: a "liberalisation" permitted to the peasants after the Cultural Revolution and much appreciated by urban consumers who benefited from higher quality and better prices than in State-run markets. 📷

复兴门内一条胡同里的国营水果店，离民族文化宫不远。（人们的）选择很有限：苹果和梨。
State-run fruit shop in an alley near Fuximenwei Avenue, not far from the Palace of National Minorities. The choice is very limited: apples and pears. 📷

西单一家电视商店，正在销售最新款的牡丹牌彩
电，当时它在中国被认为是最好的品牌。电视机
是绝大多数人所追求的物品，最终在80年代中
期得到迅速的普及。

A television shop in Xidan with the latest models
of the Mudan (Peony) brand, considered to be the
best in China. Still a sought-after item for the overwhelming majority, televisions quickly became
common in Chinese households in the late Eighties.

在景山山顶（也叫煤山）上小歇，景山位于故宫后面，就像挡风墙一样保护着故宫。从这里可以很好地欣赏故宫和整个北京城的美丽景色。唯一可以看到的现代化建筑物就是北京饭店。

A rest at the top of Jingshan Hill (also known as Coal Hill) which stands behind the Forbidden City and protects it from the wind. From here there is a wonderful view over the Imperial Palaces and the city. The only modern building standing out from the great sweep of the city is the Beijing Hotel.📷

在进故宫之前，通往午门路旁的槐树下，人们停下小歇，买点心。参观者多是普通百姓，此刻他们怀着崇敬和好奇的心情参观这座昔日皇帝住过的宫殿。

Refreshment stop before entering the Forbidden City on the avenue of acacias which leads to the Wu Men entrance. Visiting the residence of the Emperors represents almost an act of revenge for the common people; a moment, however, to be enjoyed with reverent curiosity. 📷

午门前广场的一个侧门，午门是故宫的正式入口。

One of the side entrances to Wu Men Square, Meridian Gate, the official entrance to the Forbidden City. 📷

颐和园是一处美妙的去处，距老城墙14公里，曾经是清末慈禧太后的夏天居所。如今一批批游客从城里赶来，要花费一天的时间来参观宫殿群，在昆明湖边散步，爬爬万寿山。

The Summer Palace is a delightful place, 14 km. from the old city walls, and once stood in open countryside. It was the favourite summer residence of the Empress Ci Xi. Today it draws crowds from the city who spend the whole day there, visiting the pavilions, strolling along the banks of Lake Kunming or climbing the hill of the Ten Thousand Buddhas. 📷

五一劳动节的颐和园。牌楼上挂着毛主席语录：
"工业学大庆，农业学大寨，把国民经济搞上去！"
Mayday at the Summer Palace. The words on the
pailou (triumphal arch) taken from the quotations
of Mao contain the warning: "Industry must learn
from Daqing, agriculture from Dazhai and the national economy must grow". 📷

1934—1935年红军长征时,毛泽东在一首词(清平乐·六盘山)里写到"不到长城非好汉",一次"万里长城"的游览不仅使人惊叹不已,更感到一种道义上的责任感。这是在八达岭拍的照片,这个中国在世界上最著名的古迹,可以使人们体会到"国家崇敬"的精神。

一群军人和老百姓在高兴地"攀登"长城。

下图: 在通往明十三陵的"神道"上的牧羊人和运货的马车。

In a poem written during the Long March in 1934–1935, Chairman Mao wrote, "if we do not reach the Great Wall we are not real Chinese". A trip to the "Wall of Ten Thousand Li" is thus not only a matter of curiosity but also a moral obligation. In these photographs taken at Badaling, one can feel the spirit of national reverence for the most famous historical Chinese monument in the world.

The Great Wall "climbed" by happy groups of soldiers and civilians.

Underside: Shepherds and mule-drawn carts on the "Spirit Way" leading to the Ming Tombs. 📷

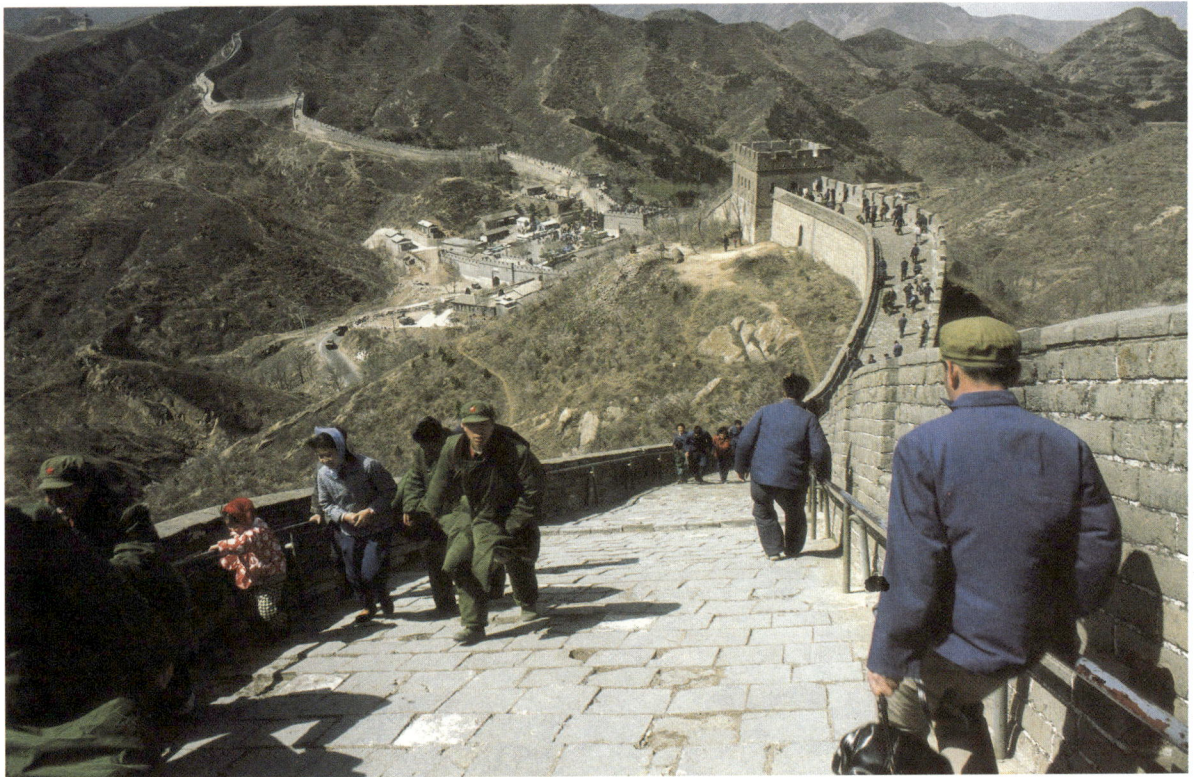

这几张照片拍摄于80年代初，我们可以看出气氛已经有明显的转变，体现在服装款式的新颖和颜色的鲜艳上；出现的商业广告牌，取代了过去的政治标语。1981年7月1日《中国日报》脱颖而出，这是英文版的日报，预示着中国对世界开放。

下图: 前门前面左侧的广告牌上，《经济日报》开始订阅，"生意"这个词汇进入了中国。

In these photographs we are at the beginning of the Eighties and the change in the atmosphere is already evident in the new styles of clothing, the brighter colours and in the appearance of commercial advertising which has substituted political propaganda. On 1 June 1981, the China Daily was published for the first time, a daily newspaper in English which preceded the opening up of China to the world.

Underside: As the advertisement behind Qianmen Gate to the left shows, a daily financial newspaper is also on sale. The word "business" has arrived in China. 📷

小贩们正在东岳庙前卖西瓜，可以看到尚存的漂亮的牌楼，是用石头和琉璃瓦制成的。

下图：在钟楼对面的鼓楼居民区，休闲的日常生活。

Selling watermelons on the pavement in front of the Dong Yue Miao Temple, with the beautiful surviving "pailou" in stone and ceramic.

Underside: Scenes of ordinary daily life on the pavement next to the Bell Tower in the bustling district of Gulou. 📷

80年代中期，服装款式变换很快，这取决于私有企业的快速发展，这些私企以生产消费品为主，特别是服装行业。

下图：天安门广场上的一个孩子，穿着很现代的服装，而老式的奶瓶里装的是茶而不是牛奶。

In the mid-Eighties styles of dress change rapidly following the explosion of private enterprise in the production of consumer goods especially in the clothing sector.

Underside: The child in Tian'anmen Square, despite his modern clothes, still has the traditional bottle of tea rather than milk. 📷

1988年是发生巨大变化的一年：我们看看右边的照片，模特儿的时装表演首次出现在政治意识形态的圣地——天安门广场。

下图：新款式很快出现在自由市场上，建国门附近的小摊上刚到的新货：印有小花的内裤和运动服。

1988 is the year of great change. As we can see on these pages, this is a boom in fashion with models making their first appearance even in Tian'anmen Square, the shrine of political ideology.

Underside: They had first been seen in the popular markets, like this one in Jianguomen, where something entirely new appeared: pants patterned with flowers and spots which interest. 📷

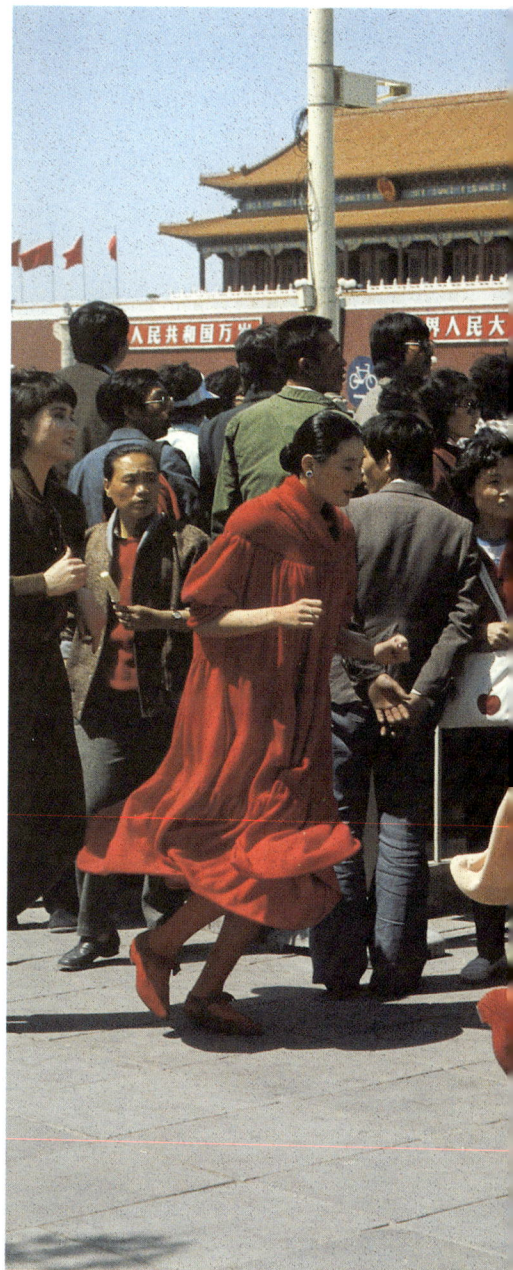

那时退休人员的消遣方式：拎着关着金丝鸟的竹
鸟笼子在日坛公园散步，会会老朋友们，举行小
鸟叫声比赛。

下图：在琉璃厂古玩一条街，两个孩子的妈妈和
姥姥在照顾他们喝酸奶。

A relaxing pastime for a pensioner: he takes his
golden orioles in bamboo cages to "Ritan", the park
of the Temple of the Sun, and awaits his friends.
The birds then compete in singing competitions.

Underside: In Liulichang, the street of the antiques
dealers, a mother and attentive grandmother are busy
encouraging two children to taste yoghurt, a great
novelty. 📷

报纸不再由邮递员递送，而是到大街上的报摊上购买。专业报刊经销商是在90年代末期出现的。

下图：古老与现代，爷爷是个非常典型的"老北京"，然而紧紧搀扶他的小孙女却非常典型地赶时髦：拉直的头发，设计时尚的毛衣，穿着高跟鞋，肩背流行手袋，嘴唇上涂着口红。

Newspapers are no longer delivered by the postman but are bought from open-air newsstands. Proper newsagents will arrive at the end of the Nineties.

Underside: Ancient and modern. The grandfather is a perfect example of old Beijing, "Lao Beijing", while his granddaughter, who is holding him tight, is an equally perfect example of modernity with a modern hair style, patterned sweater, leggings, high heels, shoulder bag and lip-stick. 📷

农历的新年, 是指中国的春节, 是中国最重要的传统节日, 春节一般是在公历一月和二月之间。除夕夜所有的家人聚集到一起会餐, 放鞭炮, 庆祝新的一年带来好运。一个妈妈, 刚刚烫完头发, 抱着半睡半醒的孩子去父母家, 手中抱着盒装的毛衣, 一派繁荣兴旺的景象。

The Chinese New Year, also known as the Spring Festival, is the most important festival in the age-old Chinese tradition and begins on the first day of the first lunar month between January and February. On the evening before the New Year families come together to eat and let off fireworks to bring good luck. A mother, fresh from the hairdresser's, arrives at her parents' with her child half asleep, carrying a packet of sweets, a sign of prosperity. 📷

春节假期里，人们涌向公园游园，品尝地摊上的油炸食品，给孩子们买农民们用竹子做的传统风车。

During the New Year holiday people flock to the parks to taste the fried foods from the temporary stalls and children are given traditional bamboo pin-wheels made by peasants. 📷

经过修复的寺院庙宇相继对游客开放，比如"雍和宫"，位于同名大街的尽头处。游客们在祭坛和菩萨前面烧香祷告，以求在刚刚开始的新年里如愿以偿。

Following their restoration, the temples are also favourite places for visitors, like the "Yong He Gong", the Temple of the Lamas, which rises at the end of the great avenue of the same name. Burning sticks of incense before the altars, with their figures of Buddha immersed in thought or offering benediction, will bring good fortune in the New Year that has just begun. 📷

新与旧的更迭（1988—1998）
The New Displaces The Old

90 年代，随着一批购物中心的建立和各种新款服装的推出，人们的生活日新月异，电影的欣赏口味大大改变：革命题材的影片在减少，取代它的是越来越多的爱情影片，或是怀旧影片。

The Nineties bring yet more changes to everyday life with the opening of department stores and all the new clothing styles. Tastes in films change too: fewer revolutionary epics and more and more love stories or stories from pre-Maoist society. 📷

90 年代末，彻底改造之前的市中心的王府井大街。

Wangfujing Street, right in the centre of the city, before its complete transformation at the end of the Nineties. 📷

裘皮服装在当时是很时髦的，特别是一些华丽、五彩缤纷的。

下图：这个小女孩儿甚至也穿着流行的大衣，系着大围巾。

Leather clothing has its part to play in the pursuit of modernity, especially if it is tied into garishly coloured clothing.

Underside: Even the little girl in the fashionable coat and the big scarf. 📷

高楼大厦淹没了北京,但是有些地方远离了现代化的狂风暴雨,像国子监里漂亮的街道,这里曾经是皇家设立的最高学府。国子监街从雍和宫大街起,经孔庙到相邻的国子监最后连接到安定门内大街。

下图: 高楼大厦群的增长无可阻挡,一些胡同破旧房屋里的居民们不由得产生对现代化住宅的向往。

The building boom is about to engulf Beijing. For the moment, a few places are spared by the frenzy of modernisation like the beautiful street of Guozijian, or Imperial College, which from the Avenue of the Temple of the Lamas leads to the Temple of Confucius and to the nearby Classical Hall, emerging into Andingmen Nei Avenue.

Underside: But the advance of the new tower blocks is unstoppable, and the humble houses of the hutung can last only so long as the inhabitants themselves yearn for modernity. 📷

明十三陵离市中心较远，现代化也将光临此地。人们的穿衣已有所改变，但仍然赶着由三匹骡子拉着的老式马车。

厚实的棉口罩并不是为了预防流感，而是由于寒冷的天气。

Modernisation will reach the Ming Tombs, a certain distance from the city, a little later. The style of dress has changed, but the man is still driving his cart in the traditional way using three mules.

The heavy cotton mask offers protection not against influenza, but against the icy air. 📷

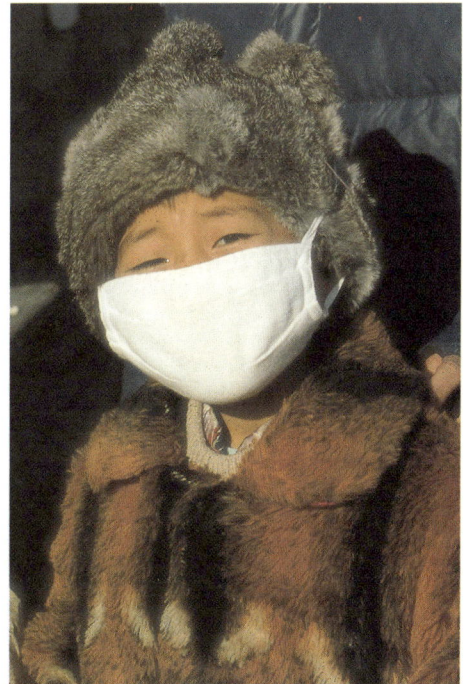

结婚是与过去决裂和建立新生活的另一种机会，照片里的那一对夫妇，他们穿着西式礼服，刚刚在一个地方政府的机构里面宣过誓。

下图：时尚的中式礼服：一对新婚夫妇在回新房前，在和亲朋好友们一起庆贺。

Marriage is another opportunity to break with the past and embark on a new life, and all the better if it is conducted in perfectly western clothes like those of the couple on the night who have just made their vows in a local town hall.

Underside: Modern but in Chinese style: the bride and groom surrounded by friends and relatives as they go up to their new flat. 📷

夏天来了，处处可见到色彩明亮的时装。

下图：1997 年 7 月 1 日香港回归中国前，人们自豪地穿着印有回归字样的 T 恤。

Come the summer, the bright colours of the new fashions can be seen everywhere.

Underside: Approaching 1ˢᵗ July 1997, when the British colony of Hong Kong is to be handed over to China, T-shirts announcing the event are worn with legitimate pride. 📷

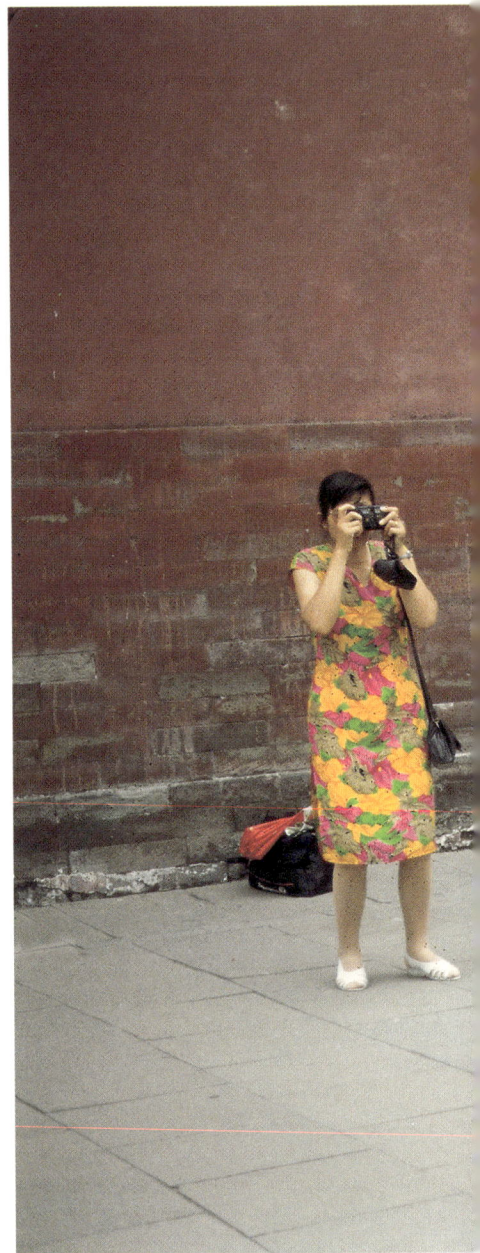

在 20 世纪结束前，从故宫开始，逐步对首都大多数历史古建筑进行维修。

下图：兄妹二人，穿着蓝色和粉色的西式传统服装，姿势有点局促地站在故宫乾清宫门前。

Before the end of the 20st century restoration work is begun on many historic buildings in the capital, beginning with the Forbidden City.

Brother and sister, dressed in blue and pink in strict accordance with western tradition, pose a little embarrassed at the entrance to the Palace of Heavenly Purity in the Forbidden City. 📷

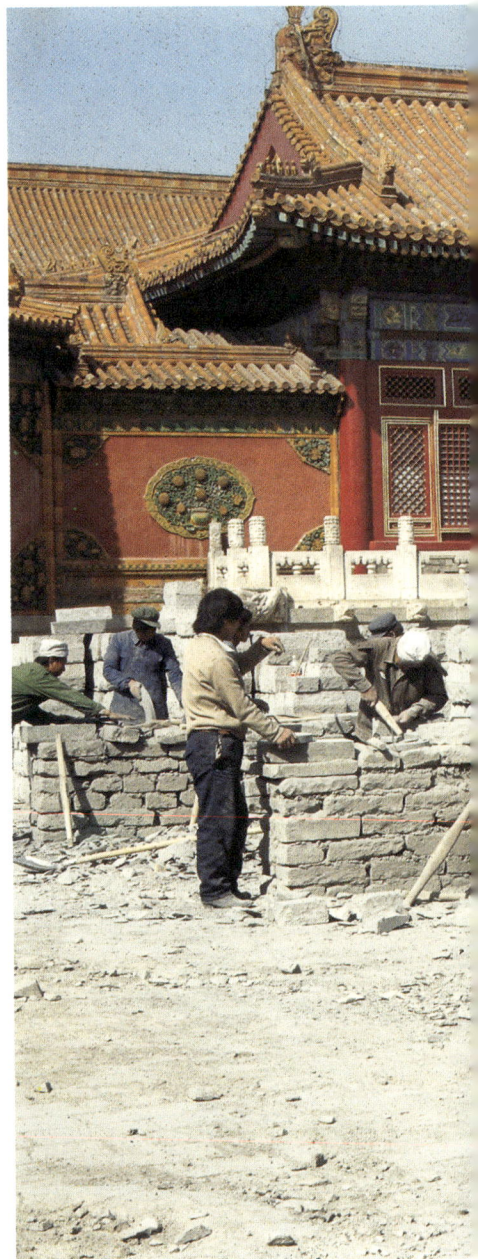

精心修复紫禁城,使其继续保持着真正的城市心脏地位,尽管北京城外貌和市民的生活习惯已经发生了变化。

The carefully restored Forbidden City continues to be the most authentically Chinese setting in the heart of a city that has so dramatically changed its appearance and in part its habits. 📷

在1994年，王府井大街上的东安市场被拆除了，1997年，它被改造成为一个新式大型综合商业中心。

老北京的胡同，包括市中心的和郊区的商业地区，为了尽快修建21世纪的新首都，大部分都被夷为平地了。

下图: 天平酒店周围的胡同里破旧的平房很快就被高楼大厦代替了。

The destruction of the Dong'an market on Wangfujing Street in 1994. By 1997 an enormous new shopping centre of the same name will be built. Vast areas of the old Beijing of the hutung, but also of the commercial districts in the centre and in the outskirts of the city, were razed to the ground to make way for the rapid construction of the 21st century capital.

Underside: The towering Hotel Tianping dominates the run-down houses of the old hutung which will shortly disappear to make way for yet more skyscrapers. 📷

与世界同步（1998—2008）

In Step With The World

建国门地区国际饭店后面的小街，2000年来临前，这里原有的建筑都被推土机铲平，取而代之的是现在看到的宽阔的大街，两旁是现代化的高楼大厦。

下图: 从南方来的建筑工人们在工地上吃着简单的午餐。

The days are numbered for the streets behind the International Hotel in Jianguomen. Before the new millennium the whole area will be bulldozed and a new wide boulevard with modern residential blocks either side will take its place.

Underside: Construction workers from the distant southern provinces eat their meagre lunch on site.

在 20 年来经济改革的作用下，人们的生活水平
有了明显的提高。2000年来临前夕，越来越多不
同打扮的中国人开始考虑外出旅游了：有一家人
到天坛游览，品尝着新制的饮料，而其他的游
客，正在大口地吃着北京面条。

The increase in living standards, although contained,
is quite evident and is the result of the economic
reforms of the last twenty years. On the cusp of the
millennium, an increasing number of Chinese, having begun to dress differently, are beginning to
travel: a family of tourists at the Temple of Heaven
enjoy the taste of new drinks, and others in a restaurant tuck into Beijing noodles. 📷

冬天，除了寒冷外，对于我来说，是北京最好的
季节。老年人和年轻人可以晒太阳，从事新的娱
乐活动，在百年柳树点缀下的北海冰冻湖面上，
滑着冰车。

The winter, which for me despite the cold is the best
season in Beijing, brings the sun and new pastimes
for young and old, with sledges on the frozen lakes
like that at Bei Hai surrounded by the delicate trac-
ery of the ancient willows. 📷

在颐和园万寿山下的昆明湖冰面上玩耍,这是冬天的娱乐活动。各种各样款式和颜色的服装变化,说明这是一场真实的革命。

下图:老人还保持着戴厚实棉手套的习惯,在天坛的东花园里散步,每周日都坐在这里听歌和看表演。

Winter games on the frozen surface of Lake Kunming at the Summer Palace, near the hill with the Temple of the Ten Thousand Buddhas. The variety of clothes and colours is in itself a genuine revolution.

Underside: Tradition, however, is maintained by the old man in his heavy gloves visiting the eastern gardens of the Temple of Heaven, the setting for Sunday shows by singers and performers. 📷

新东安市场位于重新修建的王府井大街上,离它不太远的是东堂,这是一座巴洛克建筑风格的天主教堂,建于 17 世纪。教堂前的广场侧面修建的是天伦饭店。

下图:位于东长安街上东方新天地的全景,汽车拥堵很严重,在道路两旁有专用自行车道。

The big, modern Dong'an market on a now unrecognisable Wangfujing Street. Not far away rises the Cathedral of the East, a baroque Catholic church built by Italian Jesuits in the 17th century, the courtyard of which has been turned into a public square.To the side, the Tianlun Hotel.

Underside: The Oriental Plaza on Chang'an Dong Avenue with road traffic. There are one-way cycle lanes on either side of the road. 📷

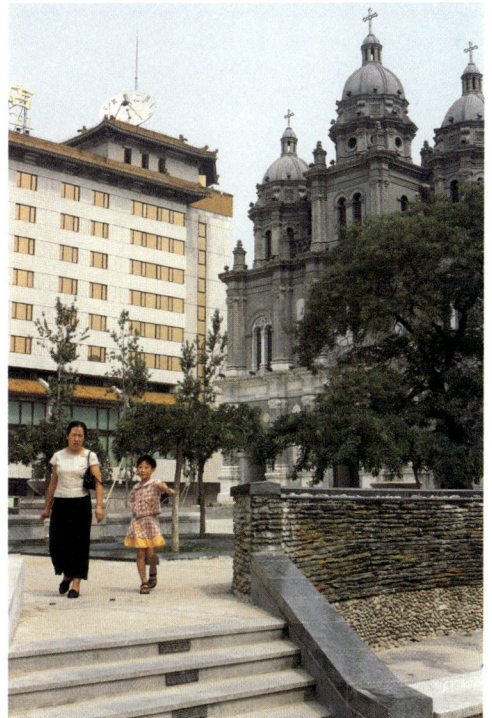

这几张照片，是王府井大街普通日常生活的一景。

On this pages, scenes of everyday life on the Wangfujing Street of today. 📷

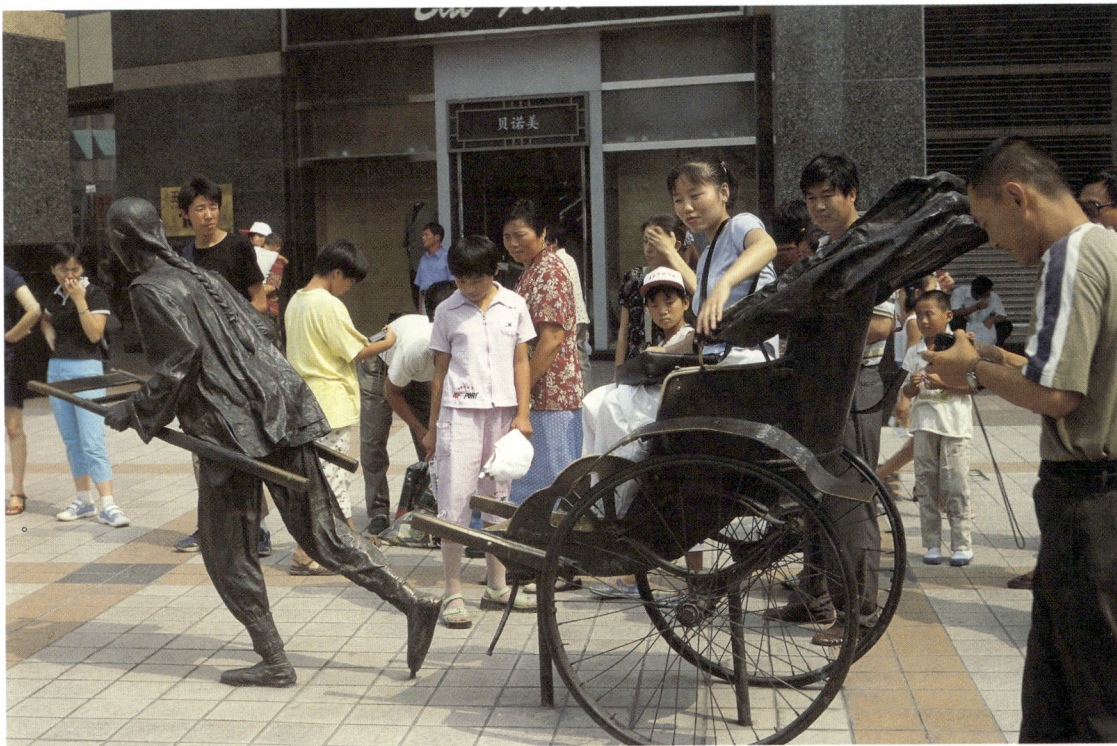

来天坛旅游的中国游客和外国游客(倚在第三层
栏杆上)。天坛是北京的象征，也是明代建筑的
精髓。

Chinese tourists, and westerners (leaning on the
third balustrade) visiting the Temple of Heaven,
which has risen to become a symbol for the city
itself, the quintessence of ancient Ming architecture.

位于奥运村的北面一个新住宅区。公寓虽小，但安装了空调。北京是世界上无论是私人住宅，还是公共建筑发展都最快的城市。

New residential areas in the northern part of the city near the Olympic Village. The apartments are small but air-conditioned. Beijing has seen the greatest growth in both private and public building of any city in the world. 📷

2008 年奥运会开幕前，一家人去天安门广场游览，在积雪堆上微笑着让他们的业余摄影师照相留念。

Waiting for the Olympic Games in 2008, a family visiting Tian'anmen Square poses on a pile of snow and waves happily to your amateur photographer who has immortalised them. 📷

新修复的前门大街，这里在过去帝王时期曾经是
北京著名的商业中心区。
The renovated area along Qianmen Dajie is now with
its heart in the glorious past of Beijing at the time
of the Empire. 📷

"北京2008"奥林匹克运动会期间,王府井大街上熙熙攘攘的人群。

People in the busiest Wangfujing Dajie during the era of the Olimpic Games "Beijing 2008". 📷

北京城象征之一的东便门角楼和明城墙遗址公园，是北京城昔日辉煌的现代见证。

The tower corner of Dongbianmen, one of the symbols of Beijing, and the park of the Ming Walls, modern witness of the glorious city past. 📷

中国现代化首都的象征，绿色奥运的"鸟巢"和"水立方"。

The "bird nest" in the Olimpic Green, symbol with the Aquatic Stadium of the modern capital of China.

超现代化的北京火车站南站，梦想成真：北京——
天津高速列车只需半个多小时即可到达。
The new super modern Railway Station "Beijing
South", one of many dreams got true: Beijing-
Tianjin in half an hour of fast train. 📷

国贸：北京东部的现代化贸易中心，周边的道路、花园、高架桥和明亮的大厦筑成了一道绚丽的城市风景。

Guomao, the modern trade center in the est side of Beijing with its charming urban landscape of roads, gardens, bridges and sparkling buildings. 📷

责任编辑：林　敏
装帧设计：曹　春

图书在版编目（CIP)数据

一个意大利记者眼中的北京(1976—2008)／（意）阿德里亚诺·马达罗(Adriano
Màdaro)著　陆辛 译 －北京：人民出版社,2008.11
ISBN 978－7－01－007427－6

Ⅰ.一...　Ⅱ.①马...②陆...　Ⅲ.改革开放－概况－北京市－1976～2008
Ⅳ.D619.1

中国版本图书馆 CIP 数据核字（2008）第 164638 号

书　　　名	一个意大利记者眼中的北京(1976—2008)
	YIGE YIDALI JIZHE YAN ZHONG DE BEIJING
著 译 者	（意）阿德里亚诺·马达罗(Adriano Màdaro)著　陆辛 译
出版发行	人民出版社
	（北京朝阳门内大街 166 号　邮编　100706）
邮购地址	100706 北京朝阳门内大街 166 号
总 经 销	人民出版社发行部
邮购电话	(010)65132886　65250042　65289539
经　　销	新华书店总店北京发行所
印　　刷	北京百花彩印有限公司印刷　新华书店经销
版　　次	2008 年 11 月第 1 版　2008 年 11 月北京第 1 次印刷
开　　本	889 毫米×1194 毫米 1/16　印张 13
字　　数	200 千字
书　　号	ISBN 978－7－01－007427－6/
定　　价	148.00 元